WILLPOWER

The Secrets
of Self-Discipline

KERRY L. JOHNSON, MBA, Ph.D.

Louis & Ford Publishing
Tustin, California

Copyright © 2003 by Kerry L. Johnson, MBA, Ph.D.
www.KerryJohnson.com

All rights reserved. No part of this book may be reproduced or transmitted in any form or by any means, electronic or mechanical, including photocopying, recording, or by any information storage and retrieval system without permission in writing from the publisher.

Published by Louis & Ford
PO Box 3665
Tustin, CA 92781
(800) 883-8787

Publisher's Cataloging-in-Publication Data on file

ISBN 0-9618535-2-2

Printed in the United States of America

Readers are raving about
Willpower: The Secrets of Self-Discipline...

Dr. Kerry Johnson is a dynamic leader whose insights make an immediate impact. By using Kerry to speak at our client meetings, we have seen our relationships with our best clients reach new levels. Kerry articulates easy to use steps in this book that anyone can translate into winning results.

KEVIN ROWELL
Managing Director, Alliance Capital

One hopes that a book has good information. *Willpower* not only provides great ideas but is also very entertaining. I wish all of my students could read it. It would make my job easier.

DR. SANDI REID
Dallas Baptist University School of Business

Tiger Woods is often thought of as the most talented golfer in the game today. The truth is he is the hardest worker. This allows him to take maximum advantage of enormous talent. *Willpower* gives all of us a step by step approach to take advantage of the skills talents we also have. This book should be read by anyone who wants to improve their game no matter what game that is.

ERIK FINN HORVE
PGA Teaching Professional

Kerry's insights in *Willpower* are invaluable. By staying self-disciplined, my clients' leadership teams successfully vision, plan and execute amidst a storm of change.

CHRISTOPHER GLEITER
Deloitte Consulting

Your chapter on developing self-disciplined kids has been extremely helpful. It is so important to allow kids to experience the consequences of their actions. Often I have tried to insulate my kids, never allowing them hardship. But self-discipline can't be learned until it is also experienced. This book is already helping my children become more responsible and self-disciplined.

>**M. JEAN MONTGOMERY**
>Mother and flight attendant

The one thing missing in learning any technique or skill is the self discipline to use it. It is not enough knowing "how" to do something. This book gets readers to actually make it happen. *Willpower* is the glue that makes all other skills come together.

>**ROGER DAWSON**
>Professional speaker and author of *Power Negotiation*

I was taught that it was not the strongest or fastest who win every time, but those with the most mental toughness. In the game of tennis, willpower and self-discipline are as important to winning as any great shot.

>**TIM PAWSAT**
>Professional Tennis Player/Teacher
>13 time National Junior Champion
>NCAA Doubles Champion
>ATP top 20 in the World Doubles Ranking

My patients include some of Hollywood's brightest stars. Yet I have noticed all of them possess one thing. An amazing degree of self-discipline. Luck comes to those who are prepared and work hard. Fame and wealth come to those who are self-disciplined. Your book should be required reading for anyone who wants to be more and achieve more in life whether it be fame, great wealth or just a better person.

>**RICK JACOBSON, DDS**
>Renowned Orthodontist
>Faculty UCLA School of Denistry

*To my beautiful daughters,
Stacey, Catherine and Caroline,
whom I am not only proud of, but also admire.
They have grown from undisciplined ravel rousing kids
to self-disciplined, poised, young ladies.
Also to my wonderful wife, Merita, who has made the
sacrifices that have held everything together.
They are all blessings from God.*

Table of Contents

Acknowledgments   ix
Introduction   1

SECRET ONE:	The Psychology of Self-Discipline	9
SECRET TWO:	Achieving Self-Discipline by Assessing Your Values, Setting Goals, and Concentrating on Outcomes	29
SECRET THREE:	Achieving Self-Discipline through Visualization and Recasting	47
SECRET FOUR:	Achieving Self-Discipline by Modeling and Using Mentors	71
SECRET FIVE:	Achieving Self-Discipline by Changing Your Beliefs	91
SECRET SIX:	Achieving Self-Discipline by Using Contracts	111
SECRET SEVEN:	Achieving Self-Discipline by Using Meta Patterns	129
SECRET EIGHT:	Achieving Self-Discipline by Coping with Stress	149
SECRET NINE:	Using Self-Discipline to Build Wealth	177
SECRET TEN:	Building Self-Discipline in Your Kids	195
SECRET ELEVEN:	Self-Discipline and Your Spiritual Walk with God	223

Acknowledgments

I have been working on *Willpower: The Secrets of Self-Discipline* for two years. Since this is a book on self-discipline, one would think the author would be able to walk the talk. But it wasn't until editor Rebecca Chown came into my life that this book came to a conclusion. She has been instrumental in keeping me on track and making the words flow. Without her it never would have happened.

I also owe thanks to my wife, Merita, who looked at the first manuscript and asked me if I were writing for graduate students. Nora Joyce's question to her husband, James, immediately came to mind: "Why don't you write books people can read?" I've always believed readers want content rather than entertainment, but Merita was able to show me that a well-written book needs both.

I also am grateful to Sheri Rieffanaugh on my staff who consistently encouraged me to complete this work. Without her constant reading and helpful hints, it would still be in my computer.

Without knowing it, my daughters Catherine, Caroline, and my eldest daughter Stacey have contributed more than they know or later will want to know to this book. Much of the testing of my ideas on how to develop self-discipline in kids was first worked out on them. I remember dining with my family at a restaurant when Catherine, then ten, excitedly told her mother and me that she had just found a quarter. I asked where and she told me it had just been lying in a fountain. The fountain was a wishing fountain, of course, and I wanted her to put it back.

When Catherine justified taking the quarter by telling me the water was low enough to reach in and pick it up, I asked her why she hadn't taken all the quarters. She said that would be dishonest. I then asked her the difference between taking one and taking all of them. She looked at me for a long time before saying she would take the quarter back, not because it was the right thing to do, but because she was getting a headache from talking to me.

I would also like to thank my brother Kevin and sister-in-law Sharon for their encouragement in reading over the rough drafts of this book and for giving me very useful ideas on how to improve it.

Last, I would like to thank most of all our Lord God in Heaven who always gently nudges me in that quiet and sometimes not-so-still voice to maintain my priorities in life and who made sure that while I struggled to complete a major project like this book, I also remembered the people in my life who depend on me for more than a paycheck.

Without God's help, nothing is possible.

Especially writing a book.

Introduction

All human beings have goals. Maybe one of yours is to lose weight. Maybe it's to develop patience with your children or your spouse. Perhaps it's to pay your bills on time. Maybe you want to increase your productivity at work. Or maybe you want to spend less and save more, or make more so you can retire early and travel the world over.

We all have goals. If striving to better ourselves is part of the human condition, goals are how we get there. The catch is, in order to achieve our goals, we need self-discipline.

You probably have heard of people who get fabulous results by sheer willpower—another word for self-discipline—alone. You can learn to use self-discipline that effectively too. The purpose of *Willpower: The Secrets of Self-Discipline* is to teach you how to commit yourself to your goals through easy-to-apply yet advanced techniques from some of the newest and most exciting research in applied psychology.

The teaching part is necessary because, as essential as self-discipline is, it rarely comes naturally. The surprising thing is that with self-discipline, almost nothing stops us. Without self-discipline, nothing helps us.

When we have self-discipline, we're in good company. All peak performers, whether in sales, management, athletics, or any other career, have a high degree of self-discipline. This is especially apparent among those old-timers who survive in big league sports long after their less disciplined opponents are forced to quit. Sports is a zero sum game. Simply put, in order for you to win, the

> *All peak performers, have a high degree of self-discipline.*

other team must lose. The major success factor that helps older athletes is their amazing degree of self-discipline.

For example, at age forty-four, Nolan Ryan was one of the best pitchers in major-league baseball history. His retirement was due in 1991 when he was scheduled to face the best team in baseball, the Oakland A's. Not only did he complete the game, he pitched a no-hitter! His achievement was the first by a man of his age in baseball history and it was probably the biggest no-hitter among the six in his career.

Was Ryan's ability to practice keen self-discipline due to an innate power that few others possess? Hardly. Ryan himself was quick to admit that without developing and honing his self-discipline, he would have gone quickly from "Who's Who" to "Who's he?" Thus, his training regimen included vigorous weight training that left younger players huffing and puffing, a stationary bike, and a water-jogging program. This kind of discipline gave him the ability to throw one-hundred-mile-per-hour fast balls.

Younger athletes who reach the heights of their game rely on self-discipline, too. Before the 2000 British Open, golfer Tiger Woods arrived at the driving range at the Bayhill Country Club in Orlando, Florida, at 5:00 A.M., waiting for daylight and armed with only one club. The local pro, Mark Brooks, walked in at 7:00 A.M., wondering how long Tiger had been there. At lunch, the pro noticed Tiger still hitting his nine iron. Late in the afternoon, the same pro was astounded to see that Tiger was still there, as he would be until the sun went down. Finally, too curious to keep quiet any longer, he asked Tiger why he was practicing only with his nine iron and why for so long?

Tiger quietly replied that he was preparing for the British Open. He was so long off the tee that all he needed on most holes on his second shot was his 9 iron. He wanted to make sure he could hit the greens consistently with it.

Tiger went on to win the 2000 British Open and the rest is history.

Introduction

Sure, Tiger is talented. He wouldn't have been able to compete unless he were. But Tiger was also known for being the hardest working golfer on the tour. He not only was intense on the course, he also spent long hours on the practice range. For Tiger and the rest of us, whatever our game, if talent is the reason we're in it, discipline is the reason we win.

I am a speaker and author, but I was trained as a research psychologist. This means that the kinds of ideas I like to study are based on research, peppered with useful, tangible ideas that work instead of someone's opinions. Consequently, this is the type of book I like to write. Many books are available on self-discipline, but without exception they've left me wanting more. At best, these books whet the appetite. At worst, they become boring. Most of them are either too simplistic or are unrealistic, advising readers to change in ways that don't make common sense. My goal in writing *Willpower: The Secrets of Self-Discipline* is to provide ideas that can be used immediately as well as over the long haul.

> *If talent is the reason we're in it, discipline is the reason we win.*

Back in the 1980s when I was working on my Ph.D., my life consisted of reading and research with precious little time for a movie or a date. I was twenty-four years old and had few responsibilities, so I could handle such pressure relatively easily. When I started my MBA mid-career, not only did I have to run a company with twenty employees, I also had to spend enough time at home to keep my wife happy and attend to two beautiful daughters. That tight rope was not an easy one to walk. Juggling many responsibilities is tough. I mention this because I live with the same problems and concerns as you.

I have studied until 3:00 A.M. because I didn't have time during the day. I have traveled three thousand miles to give a speech when I should have been in bed with the flu. I have met payrolls when I had to borrow the funds. I have consumed protein powder drink in lieu of chewable food because I wanted to lose six inches around the middle. I have had to periodically quit drinking coffee because it created anxiety attacks. Like you, I have to make self-discipline work in my life every day.

I recently had lunch in Traverse City, Michigan, with my friend and editor Rebecca Chown. Impulsively, I asked our server what she would like to read in a self-discipline book. She replied that she worked two jobs to make ends meet and had three kids to provide for, as well as a mortgage and a car payment to meet. In short, she had precious little time to read, though any advice I could give her to add more hours in the day would be nice.

I couldn't help but wonder whether, if she had more hours, she would be more self-disciplined or would find her additional time used up without having accomplished more? I ask this because studies show that most adults watch four hours of television per day. In addition, the average adult spends forty-five minutes commuting to and from work each day.

Contrast this with the average four minutes per day we spend communicating with our spouses or our kids. "Communication" is defined as spending time talking instead of engaging in superficial conversation like giving instructions or commands. We are all pressed for free time, but if we had the free time we desire, what would we do with it?

I've just completed my MBA. It was hard to find time to work on assignments while I traveled, so I tried to catch pockets of time like studying in ticket lines or while waiting to board aircraft or while waiting for luggage. I arrived in Dallas once for a speech and was in the back of a taxi working on an assignment when the taxi driver started to complain about how long he had to wait at the airport for a fare. He said he spent three hours in the taxi holding areas every day with nothing to do. I told him I wished I had

Introduction

three hours to work on my MBA every day. He then started to complain about his low pay and long hours in the cab. I asked him if he had a college degree. He said no. I told him that college grads make on average forty thousand dollars per year more than high school grads and that he could do all his coursework waiting for fares. He laughed and said he had better things to do with his time.

The point is, do we need more time or do we need to be more disciplined with the time we have? Since there are only twenty-four hours in a day, the answer is obvious. We need self-discipline, and we need to use it like we would a tool. This tool needs to be as dependable as a good car yet as comfortable as a great pair of shoes. But be warned: Like every pair of new shoes, self-discipline may not feel so good in the beginning.

In spite of that irritating fact, if we work through the discomfort and consciously build self-discipline much as we would a muscle, it will

Do we need more time or do we need to be more disciplined with the time we have?

be ready when we need it. If we only think about self-discipline when we are in jeopardy of missing a deadline or at some other time that tests us, we will be largely unsuccessful. If we can make self-discipline a part of our daily lives, it will become effortless, a part of who we are.

Oprah Winfrey is arguably the most talented entertainer in America. She is also the wealthiest female celebrity. Talented, yes. Self-disciplined also, to a degree. But she has been unable to maintain the level of self-discipline in her personal life that she maintains in her professional life. Once able to lose seventy pounds, she displayed her new body in a nationally televised show hauling along a kid's wagon full of fat. She even unsuccessfully tried to pick up that heavy bag during one of her shows. Yet, months later, she gained much of her weight back. She is smart, talented, and motivated, but even a well known and beloved celebrity is in need of techniques to maintain self-discipline.

Willpower: The Secrets of Self-Discipline explains these techniques thoroughly but concisely. It also contains two extra chapters, the first on how to teach self-discipline to children. The greatest gifts to our youth do not lie in a trust fund or a new car for graduation. They lie in education and a level of self-discipline sufficient to enjoy the benefits of that education.

If our children can learn the lessons of self-discipline, they will do better in school and will avoid making the same mistakes less self-controlled kids tend to make. In addition, kids who are controlled, focused, and guided keep those lessons in their hearts and minds forever.

> *Kids who are controlled, focused, and guided keep those lessons in their hearts and minds forever.*

The final chapter of the book explores how to use self-discipline in our spiritual lives. Eighty-five percent of Americans who believe in a higher power claim they are Christian, ten percent Jewish, and the rest a mixture of Buddhist, Moslem, and Taoist. But what is it that supports our faith? The answer lies in the level of self-discipline we bring to it.

What part of your spiritual walk do you need to strengthen? Your prayer time? Your commitment to raising your kids in a godly household? Your faith? Your connection to the natural world?

When we really get down to who we are, it's all about character, values, and morality. I once heard character defined as what we do when nobody is watching. You would not likely steal from a department store, but would you return a wallet you found on the street? You certainly wouldn't allow your kids to lie to you, but would you tell them to lie about their ages to get a discount? The rubber meets the road when adolescents are tempted to have sex or consume alcohol or other drugs. Will they have the self-discipline or strength of character to abstain? Truly, character in great part is a result of self-discipline.

This book is easy to use. You can read the chapters in the order they are presented or you can skip around and read the chapters that most appeal to you first. All of the techniques work, and I encourage you to try them all. You may be surprised at how effective these ideas can be no matter what the application.

Each chapter ends with a section called "Assignments: Putting Self-Discipline to Work" which does just that—it gives brief assignments that will aid you in developing the good habits you need in order to develop self-discipline in your life.

There is an adage in the sales business that nothing is accomplished until something is sold. There should be a similar saying about life, along the lines of, "Nothing worth having ever came easy; nothing is accomplished without self-discipline." If you apply the following techniques, you will never again be a victim to your lack of willpower. You will be a victor over your own temptations, appetites, and vices and will learn how to live life more abundantly.

Learning the secrets of self-discipline *can* change your life. Why not get started today?

SECRET
one

The Psychology of Self-Discipline

> *Pain is the difference between what is and what you want it to be.*
>
> Spencer Johnson

John Harrison was diagnosed with pancreatic cancer at age forty-six and given six months to live. When his doctors in Chicago told him to go home and get his affairs in order, he refused.

He did some research, found the best clinic in the country for treating his cancer, and found a team of doctors who wouldn't give up on him.

Today, fourteen years later, he's going strong. Is he cancer free? No. The pancreas has been partially removed but the cancer is now in his liver. With numerous rounds of chemotherapy and radiation under his belt, he's had plenty of days when he felt sick enough to die, but he's going strong. He looks good, mostly feels good, works hard, and plays harder.

Always a man who gave back to the community and to his family, John has refused to let his cancer beat him. That means he won't allow it to harden him, make him cynical, make him selfish. A charismatic orthodontist who often straightens teeth to the beat of Rod Stewart, he gives boatloads of money away, quietly and inconspicuously lending a hand whenever someone in his small town is downtrodden.

What's more, his amazing optimism and joy in life remain unequaled. This has always been a man who loved to make himself sweat, who loved to push himself higher and harder. He still does. He laughs more than anyone else, probably cries more too, but he simply won't let his cancer get in the way of his being the best human being he can be. He wants to be at the top of the mountain every day—and he wants to get there under his own steam.

The fear gets him sometimes, but he somehow pushes it away. He's always had self-discipline—he's an athlete for heaven's sake, a top amateur tennis player—but the kind of self-discipline he needs to keep his fear under control is truly phenomenal.

As always, he continues to set the standard for the rest of us.

ANONYMOUS

Self-discipline. Either you have it or you don't, right?

Wrong. Everyone can be taught the skills and techniques to bring self-discipline into their lives. It begins by understanding the psychology of self-discipline. One of its main components is mental toughness.

Mental Toughness

Former Dallas Cowboys defensive back Bill Bates was told his first year in pro football that he was too slow, too small, and had no talent. But as a seven-year veteran of the National Football League, he refused to listen to his critics. Today, Bates believes his success is due to his mental toughness. This "steeling of the mind" is what gave him the self-discipline to achieve his goals.

Self-Talk

Each of us can increase our own "mental toughness" by monitoring how we talk to ourselves. Sports hypno-therapist Pete Siegel writes that we tend to remember everything we tell ourselves. Unfortunately, he also mentions that roughly seventy-five percent of what we tell ourselves is negative and thus works against us.

Shad Helmstetter writes much the same in his book, *What Do You Say When You Talk to Yourself?* According to Helmstetter, we humans rationalize losing our motivation to meet our goals.

Imagine this scenario: Say you go on a diet and make good progress for about one day, then hunger creeps in and you decide that the pain of not eating isn't worth the pleasure of fitting into that size eight skirt. After all, you can always start dieting next week, and this week really isn't a good time with all the work you have to do.

Soon enough, your dream of a svelte 130-pound frame that draws attention from across the street is only a pipe dream.

No wonder. A litany of "It hurts," "It's not worth it," and "This isn't a good time" would send anyone off their diet and into the cupboard to grab six Twinkies and a bottle of pop.

Compare this damaging self-talk to the more effective internal communication that can get you through the extra effort you need to meet your goal: "This exercise is painful, but it's only ten more minutes and I am on my way to losing fifteen pounds." Or, "I really crave pasta right now. This diet shake doesn't taste good. But I can just see what I will look like in two weeks. It's only two weeks out of my life. I can deal with that."

This is the kind of self-talk that keeps you on track instead of breaking down your will. Motivational consultant Dave Grant, when asked how he keeps from thinking negative thoughts, said thinking positively doesn't mean omitting negatives from your mind. Rather, Grant believes it is acceptable to allow yourself to think such thoughts but then you must replace them. When something negative comes to mind, he recommends flooding your brain with positive thoughts such as, "I'm bright, I like to be around people, I'm good looking, and I can solve any problem, any time." Negative thoughts, Grant says, will simply go away if not reinforced.

To put it another way, as Yogi Berra once said, "Half this game is ninety percent mental."

Attitude

Closely related to self-talk is attitude. My brother Kevin has an amazingly positive attitude and often asks me questions on the golf course such as, "Do you think I can hit the ball with this three wood 230 yards from behind a tree and have it land on the green?" He succeeds surprisingly often, in great part because he sets himself up for success beforehand with positive self-talk.

Pattern Interrupt

A technique that can help you interrupt your pattern of negative self-talk is called pattern interrupt. Put a rubber band around your wrist and every time you become self-critical, snap it. For instance, if you miss a deadline at work, your tendency might be to berate yourself. Snap the rubber band—it will interrupt your pattern of self-punishment. Then replace the negative talk by saying, "I know I can turn things in promptly and will the next time. I have the ability. I know I can do better." Regardless of what your goal is, use positive self-talk to help increase your mental toughness and thus your self-discipline.

Jason Wood, upon his drafting to the Dallas Mavericks, said, "We're going to turn this team around 360 degrees." Now that's the kind of attitude that gets things done.

Pleasure and Pain

The second main component of the psychology of self-discipline is understanding the pleasure/pain principle. In a nutshell, our ability to be self-disciplined depends on the pleasure or pain we associate with certain activities. Indeed, our tendency to avoid punishment and seek rewards is the prime psychological motivation for everything we do. We work for rewards that include such things as money, recognition, or status. We're polite to people because we want them to like us. Often, and this can be tough to take, our children phone us from college because they need money and not because they especially want to talk to us.

When my daughter Stacey was a freshman at James Madison University, majoring in business and communications, she would call once or twice a week and I began suspecting her of only calling when she needed money. Once she called when I was in a rush. As soon as I heard her voice, I said, "How much do you want?" She became indignant that I thought she only called when she needed money. I apologized and listened to her talk about her week and how much reading she had to do. After about twenty minutes, I told her I had to go to a meeting and she sprang to the real point of the conversation: "Dad, I really need two hundred dollars for a new dress!"

I once mentioned to an audience the notion that we are primarily motivated to earn rewards and avoid punishment and a woman raised her hand and said, "That's not true. I am a United Way volunteer." I replied that she was a United Way volunteer because she found it personally rewarding.

Determining how we personally cope with the pleasure and pain of life is the first step toward using pleasure to our advantage and keeping our fear of pain under control so that we can implement self-discipline in our lives.

Take the short quiz below to determine whether you're pleasure focused or avoidance-of-pain focused:

Your Focus: Pleasure or Pain?

1. If you are in the middle of a project, will you spontaneously take time off for a friend (pleasure focused) or do you feel compelled to stay and complete the project because you perceive some kind of punishment will occur if you don't (avoidance-of-pain focused)?
2. Do you eat only the foods you like best on your plate at dinner (pleasure focused) or do you eat at least some of all the foods because you fear that if you don't, you will suffer in some way (avoidance-of-pain focused)?
3. Do you work on projects only at the last minute when you are in a panic to get them done (pleasure focused) or do you begin projects early so that there's no way you'll miss a deadline and get in trouble (avoidance-of-pain focused)?
4. When you awaken in the morning, do you get up only when you hear a chiding voice inside your head telling you to (pleasure focused) or do you typically arrive at

work at 7:00 A.M., even though you're not a morning person, so you will be able to complete your work even if unexpected problems arise (avoidance-of-pain focused)?
5. Do you tend to do a mediocre job on things you don't like so that you can get to the "fun" projects or aspects of projects more quickly (pleasure focused) or do you typically do a conscientious job on all projects or aspects of projects, even those you don't particularly care for, in order to avoid "getting caught" (avoidance-of-pain focused)?

It doesn't take much to learn if you are pleasure or pain focused. If you answered "yes" to the pleasure focus questions more often than the avoidance-of-pain focused ones, you may be someone who is more attracted to pleasure. If your answers yield an attraction more to the avoidance of pain, it may take more than rich rewards to get you to achieve your goals; it may in fact take a perceived threat or loss to make you get moving.

Procrastination

Whether you're pleasure focused or avoidance-of-pain focused, like most individuals in the world, you probably procrastinate from time to time. Why? Simply put, when we perceive that something is going to cause us pain, we procrastinate.

Have you ever put off finishing an assignment for someone and, when it came due, told a white lie about it in an effort to gain more time to complete it? Have you ever shuffled paper around your desk instead of making an important phone call, watched a sitcom instead of reading to the kids, or spent time in the middle of your business day opening mail, even when you knew it would be more efficient and effective to read it in the late afternoon or during lunch?

Usually we feel guilty about procrastinating, but procrastination is not only an unfortunate behavior, it can also cost us business. Being late, for example, is a form of procrastination. Seventeen years ago as an aspiring consultant, I was twenty minutes late to an appointment with a customer. As this was before the days of car phones, I couldn't call ahead and warn him so I just showed up late. My customer entered the waiting room and told me that if I didn't have the courtesy of arriving on time, he wouldn't extend me the courtesy of seeing me. I learned my lesson on the spot, but it cost me thousands of dollars in revenue.

> *When we perceive that something is going to cause us pain, we procrastinate.*

There are many reasons for procrastination. The most salient are avoiding discomfort, a feeling of insecurity that you don't have the information or skill to do the task, and the illusion that the task is simplistic enough that there is no rush to start now.

A few years ago, I was assigned a deadline for writing a book. When the publisher asked me if I could keep to the schedule, I said, "Sure." After all, I had about four months to do the outline and another month to actually come up with a rough draft. But as you might have guessed, I waited until the week before the outline deadline to even start the project. I then waited until three weeks before the rough draft deadline to put pen to paper. The project was completed, but to this day I wonder what would have happened if I had given myself time to do the best job that I could. As I procrastinated beginning the project, I felt terrible. I knew I was capable of doing a great job, but I didn't give myself enough time to do it. I allowed myself to be fooled into thinking that as soon as I had done the research, I could start writing. Problem was, I even procrastinated doing the research.

Sometimes people engage in avoidance behaviors because of aversive conditioning. For example, if you've ever been thrown from a horse, you may have been conditioned by this experience to never ride again. Likewise, if you've ever been on a diet and failed, you may have been aversely conditioned to never diet again.

Whatever its origins, procrastination often keeps us from doing what we need—and frequently want—to do. Since procrastination is really a result of focusing on the pain of a task instead of on its benefits, why not simply restructure how we perceive the pain and the benefits?

Here are three simple steps that can literally restructure your associations, moving a given activity from pain to pleasure. It follows that eventually the activity itself will become less painful if you remember to follow these steps.

Three Steps to Restructure Your Pleasure/Pain Associations

1. **Make a picture, sound, or feeling representation of your goal and try to experience the result of the task at hand before you even start it.** For example, try to visualize a clean garage instead of how much effort it will take to get it that way. Focus on how much easier it will be to find the things you need, park the car, or just have the ability to move in the garage without being hit in the head by unidentified falling objects.
2. **Intensify your perception of the good experience until the prospect of completion brings a smile to your face.** Continue to intensify what you see, hear, and feel. Make the garage you've been putting off cleaning so bright it is blindingly clean. That should make you smile, especially if you haven't touched it in years.
3. **Drop everything and start the activity immediately.** You don't have to complete it; just do enough to change your emotions. Straighten up one corner of the

garage, then congratulate yourself. Write a cover letter or an opening statement for a report and then stop, or make one of those phone calls you've been putting off.

One other extremely effective technique for overcoming procrastination is to use the four basic steps of planning, learning, observing, and engaging.

Planning, Learning, Observing, Engaging

1. **Planning**. One of the most common ways you can sabotage yourself is by failing to begin a project. You have likely heard in the past that "Inch by inch, anything's a cinch." The hardest part is the first inch. You can make that first inch easier if you sit down and make a game plan of the project you wish to complete. Suppose you have a speech to give two weeks from today. You wouldn't wait until the last day to start preparing, or would you?

In the most desirable of situations, you'd first plan the major portion of your talk. You'd think about the purpose and whom you'd be speaking to. Then you'd plug in the points that illustrated each idea. Next you might put in some humorous stories to illuminate your concepts. You'd probably jot some notes about where you might need to look for additional information. You'd also schedule practice time in order to give your presentation a dry run.

Planning is easy in the context of a speech, but it helps to combat self-doubt and procrastination in other areas, too. Once you start the process by engaging in an activity as simple as making a plan, you'll find it much easier to complete what you've been putting off.

2. **Learning**. Second, write down what you will have to do or learn in order to complete the project. We often feel paralyzed and procrastinate because we don't know what to do first. Recently I was assigned the task of writing a series

of articles for a major magazine. I wasn't as familiar with the topic as I would have liked, so as I planned out the project I put a checkmark next to the areas that needed more research. During the next few weeks, I found myself talking to many people about the topic and even thinking about it on my way to work in the morning. I spent time researching the issues I was confused about and noticed that most of my initial confusion simply evaporated.

This is a side benefit of planning early. On the flip side, if you wait to start any part of your project until the day it is due, you will not be able to let your mind automatically solve problems for you. It is said that Thomas Edison encountered many problems during his research on creating the light bulb. Often when stuck, he would leave his lab and take a short nap. When he awoke, he frequently had a solution to the problem.

3. **Observing**. What is it that keeps you from arriving on time to appointments and causes you to avoid easy chores like balancing your checkbook? Take out a sheet of paper and list the emotional benefits you receive from procrastinating. If this sounds like a silly exercise, think again. I tried this to help solve my problem of tardiness and was surprised to learn that I have an intense loathing towards having to wait. The thought of sitting in someone's office reading a useless magazine until the customer wrangles enough time to see me causes me acute anxiety. As a result, I typically only give myself the exact time I think it will take me to travel. Unfortunately, I rarely estimate real drive time and traffic delays well so I frequently am late. All this, thanks to my fear of waiting.

4. **Engaging**. The last step in overcoming procrastination is to engage yourself in your goal. This simply means that you're attempting to start it. As mentioned above, simply taking the first step works amazingly well to get you moving

in the right direction. I have completed many major projects with the initial plan of doing only a few minutes of work. In every case, I've ended up completing the job.

The most productive achievers work a little each day on important projects, even if only to open a folder and review what they have done so far. If you engage yourself in doing something with a high degree of frequency, there is absolutely no way you will be able to put it off for long.

Fears

A second aspect of the pleasure/pain principle that is irrevocably intertwined with the expectation of pain involves the fears we humans experience, from the fear of rejection to the fear of looking foolish to the fear of failure or even the fear of success. Whatever the source of our fears, they destroy self-discipline. While we've spent a lifetime learning such fears, they're irrational.

Fear of Failure

Take the fear of failure. Living a self-disciplined life does not mean living without failure. Even the most disciplined people alive face challenges and pitfalls, but they know how to triumph over them or at least to rise above them.

Often, misfortune can be a great teacher. When you fail, you learn volumes about what you do well and what you need to work on. Your strengths and abilities as well as your weaknesses are put in proper perspective. Interestingly enough, some researchers believe that those who don't fail enough are actually sleeping their way through life, taking too few risks, while those who fail and learn from their losses are usually the individuals most likely to succeed later.

As mentioned above, Thomas Edison struggled to find a filament for his light-burning device. None would last more than a couple of seconds before it was consumed. When one doubter told him he had failed, he responded that, on the contrary, he had found ten thousand methods that didn't work.

To use a more modern example, a salesperson I knew feared she would be unable to complete an advanced sales course. The program would have helped her increase her ability to sell to prospects in more affluent markets, but she felt that if she failed to complete the course successfully, she wouldn't be able to handle the rejection from her associates. She already doubted her abilities and wasn't willing to risk her self-confidence further if she didn't complete the course.

> *Those who fail and learn from their losses are usually the individuals most likely to succeed later.*

Predictably, her avoidance behavior prevented her from advancing her sales ability and production. She admitted later that if she'd done the training, she would have increased her income by $100,000 per year.

Another entrepreneur who was contacting people to introduce his services confessed that he frequently told his potential customer's *assistant* about his service, thinking this individual would help him get in the door. Of course, his closing rate was low because he was essentially depending on the assistant to sell for him. I asked him why and discovered that he didn't want to be rejected by the decision-maker. It was less painful if the assistant rejected him.

The problem, in sales anyway, is that most new business comes from those who have rejected you before. Most salespeople will stop after the first no and rarely will they risk being told no three times, but those who make the real money are magnets for rejection. They consequently are paid well for it.

I experienced irrational fear when I began my speaking career. After finishing graduate school, I wanted to stay in applied psychology in some way yet the academic teaching competition was stiff and fellowships were few and far between. I also didn't relish working in academia any longer. So I started to speak to associations and professional groups as a way of advertising my consulting skills. Unfortunately, I was too young to be taken credibly and I was rarely asked to consult. But I was flooded with speaking requests. I guess they thought I could do less damage speaking than through extensive consulting engagements.

> *Most new business comes from those who have rejected you before.*

The problem was, I was so terrified of speaking in front of groups that I was unable to sleep a wink before a speech for two years. To this day, I feel my biggest achievement has been overcoming that fear.

Progressive Collapse

A great way to deal with the fear of failure is to use a technique called progressive collapse in which you imagine yourself going through the steps of a total and complete collapse. For example, if you are overweight and finally enroll in a diet therapy program yet also decide it would be difficult to risk failure, you'd think of all the bad things that could happen. You would first say to yourself, "If I don't lose the weight, I'll feel upset."

You'd then hear a voice inside your head say, "What then?"

"Well, then I'll be depressed," you'd answer.

The voice would ask, "What then?"

"Then I'll probably be irritated with myself," you'd respond.

"What then?"

"I'll probably eat more," you'd answer.

"What then?"

"I guess I'll eventually try another weight loss program."

By carrying this to an extreme, you're suddenly faced with the reality that the worst that can happen isn't all that bad. In fact, it's not as frightening as you thought. Progressive collapse forces you to take a realistic look at the worst that could happen rather than to indulge in a nightmarish illusion that becomes real because it's never challenged.

Eliminate "Failure" from Your Vocabulary

In addition to using the technique of progressive collapse, try the technique of putting failure in perspective by deleting it from your vocabulary altogether. Don't say the word, think it, or listen to others who say it. See only results from what you do, some of them positive, some of them negative, all of them educational. And remember that top business people don't use the word "failure." Instead they use words like "setback," "correction," or "modification."

Force Yourself to Fail

You might also consider the novel idea of *forcing* yourself to fail to help you realize once and for all that it's not fatal. Some colleges actually offer courses in failure, assigning projects that are guaranteed to go wrong so that people can learn to desensitize themselves from emotional paralysis when failure happens in the real world.

Fear of Success

While many self-sabotaging fears exist, one of the most insidious and confusing is the fear of success. We'd all do well to remember Oscar Wilde's famous quote regarding success: "There are only two tragedies in life: One is not getting what one wants, and the other is getting it."

To use a benign example, say you're on the tee of the eighteenth hole, the last one to drive. If you can just maintain your lead, you'll have bragging rights until the next outing. You position yourself over the ball, lining up your head and feet perfectly, draw your club back, and follow through staring down the fairway. But instead of seeing your ball in flight, you hear the laughter of your friends behind your back because you've totally missed the ball.

Whoops. Fear of success strikes again.

> *Identify how the fear is represented in your mind, then change it.*

Other examples aren't so harmless. A salesman recently told me that he seemed to be limiting himself to making about $40,000 a year. When I asked why he wasn't growing in his career, he mentioned that his father was a teacher with a master's degree who only made $25,000 a year. This salesperson had only a high school graduation certificate. He felt so guilty about making more money than his father that he put off building his career and sabotaged his income.

Diminished Intensity

A technique called diminished intensity works well to decrease the power of irrational fears, including the fear of success. To use it, identify how the fear is represented in your mind, then change it. For example, a salesman recently told me that he doesn't like face-to-face prospecting with professional business people because of the intense fear of rejection he feels. It's so debilitating for him that he totally freezes up when he's in front of high-income prospects.

I taught him to picture himself seated alone in a movie theater. I told him to see himself on the screen in a movie acting out the troubling experience. After he watched the experience unfold, he played it backwards as if he were rewinding a video player. Then he played it forwards, but this time he put his favorite music to it and increased the speed of the movie. When he got to the end, he again played it backwards, making it appear to be a comical slapstick routine. The experience worked to desensitize him to the panic he normally felt.

Interrupt Your Fear

Simply interrupting your fear while you're in the middle of it can be effective, too. For example, think of the last time you felt rejected by someone. It could have been a pretty woman you wanted to ask out, or maybe your boss turned down your request for a raise, or maybe your husband failed to compliment the new bathing suit you spent three hours picking out. Remember the anxiety you felt. Now immediately stand up and walk around for a moment.

Anxiety takes a lot of concentration to maintain. If you can't be attentive, your fear goes away. The obvious suggestion is that if you feel one of your fear patterns is interfering with the discipline you need to control your emotions, do something to interrupt it.

My wife Merita became a flight attendant even though she had a fear of heights. When a job with AirCal (which became American Airlines through a merger) came up, she saw the way out of her dead-end bank job. Instead of focusing on the panic she knew she would feel for the first few flights, she concentrated on the glamour of traveling to far-off places she might never have had the chance to otherwise see.

While controlling anxiety can be difficult, psychological researcher Rollo May believes that some anxiety

> *There is a very thin line between anxiety that paralyzes and the breed of stress that helps you win.*

can actually be good. The problem is, there is a very thin line between anxiety that paralyzes and the breed of stress that helps you win.

Golfer Payne Stewart won the U.S. Open in 1999 with a twenty-foot putt on the last hole. Phil Michelson, his closest competitor, had been making amazing putts the whole day except on the seventeenth hole, where he missed an easy five-footer. If not for that missed putt, Phil could have forced a play-off with Stewart and possibly won his first major tournament.

A reporter asked Michelson if he felt the pressure on the last few holes. He said yes. When asked the same question, Stewart said that he felt anxiety but that he was able to control it.

Controlling it. Maintaining self-discipline. That's what it's all about.

Staying Self-Disciplined—the Final Word

A manager recently told me that if he could just motivate his salespeople, profits would skyrocket.

We have to realize that everyone is motivated, whether it's to sit at home in the evenings watching sitcoms or to shop every day of the week or to work on a myriad of other projects or objectives. Being motivated is not the issue. Restructuring objectives and understanding how we handle our perceptions of pleasure and pain are what motivation—or self-discipline—is all about.

The answer to losing weight lies in self-discipline and learning to change the way we perceive the pain and pleasure of dieting.

Nutritionists say that the average overweight person goes on 1.5 diets annually and tries more than fifteen times to lose weight, all between the ages of twenty-one and fifty. Predictably, most diets fail.

Stanford researchers also report that most overweight people do not seek professional help, and those who do often drop out of their weight loss regimen without losing much weight. The reason is simple: They are unable to continue the dieting program because of the pain involved in trying to stay on a plan, especially if the plan has previously failed for them.

These same researchers have added a new twist to an already sad story: Surveying a ten-year period of medical treatment for obesity, they calculated the percentage of patients who lost significant amounts of weight and found that no more than twenty-five percent lost as much as twenty pounds and no more than five percent lost as much as forty pounds. They also said that those who lost the weight often gained most of it back within a short period of time.

The reason, again, is the pain of staying committed. Losing weight is tough for most people, but it does not have to be. The answer to losing weight lies in self-discipline and learning to change the way we perceive the pain and pleasure of dieting, or any other challenge we accept.

Truly, the answer to all such dilemmas lies in understanding the power of mental toughness and the pleasure/pain principle or, in other words, the psychology of self-discipline.

ASSIGNMENTS

Putting Self-Discipline to Work

1. Think about how you respond to stressful situations. What is your attitude? In short, do you have mental toughness? Use the technique of pattern interrupt to help yourself use positive self-talk.
2. To begin confronting your natural tendency to avoid pain, change the order in which you deal with life's demands. For example, try eating the food you like least first at breakfast, lunch, and dinner. When you get

to work tomorrow morning, try doing the most distasteful job you face first. This should be an activity like filing that you've been postponing because it's uncomfortable or just plain isn't fun.

3. Take a few moments and write down three things you know you should do but haven't. This could be anything from pruning trees to doing a performance review to challenging your habit of swearing. Next to these items, write down the expectation of discomfort and pain that's contributing to your procrastination.

   Now jot down the pleasure you'll receive as a result of completing these tasks. This could be a financial reward, praise, or even a sense of pride from having done something you are proud of.

   Then use the three-step process to restructure the pleasure/pain you associate with these tasks. Also use the technique of planning, learning, observing, and engaging to overcome the procrastination you normally employ as related to these activities.

4. Make a list of the irrational fears you have and use the techniques explained in this chapter to deal with them. Try the technique of progressive collapse to deal with the fear of failure. Delete the word "failure" from your vocabulary and see what happens. Use the technique of diminished intensity on another fear, as well as the technique of interrupting your fear to see what happens. Depending on how advanced your fears are, you may even want to consider the benefits of forcing yourself to fail.

SECRET
two

Achieving Self-Discipline by Assessing Your Values, Setting Goals, and Concentrating on Outcomes

> *If you don't know where you are going, you might wind up someplace else.*
>
> Yogi Berra

When she looked ahead, Florence Chadwick saw nothing but a solid wall of fog. She had been swimming for nearly sixteen hours and her body was numb. Already she was the first woman to swim the English Channel in both directions. Now, at age thirty-four, her goal was to become the first woman to swim from Catalina Island to the California coast.

On that Fourth of July morning in 1952, the sea was like an ice bath and the fog was so dense she could hardly see her support boats. Sharks cruised toward her lone figure, only to be driven away by rifle shots. Against the frigid grip of the sea, she struggled on, hour after hour, while millions watched on national television.

Alongside Florence in one of the boats, her mother and trainer offered encouragement. They told her it wasn't much farther. But all she could see was fog. They urged her not to quit. She never had . . . until then. With only a half mile to go, she asked to be pulled out.

Still thawing her chilled body several hours later, she told a reporter, "Look, I'm not excusing myself, but if I could have seen land I might have made it." It was not fatigue or even the cold water that had defeated her. It was the fog. She had been unable to see her goal.

Two months later, she tried again. This time, despite the same dense fog, she swam with her faith intact and her goal clearly pictured in her mind. She knew that somewhere behind that fog was land and this time she made it! Florence Chadwick became the first woman to swim the Catalina Channel, eclipsing the men's record by two hours!

ANONYMOUS

While there are many ways to go about achieving self-discipline, one of the best is by doing what Florence Chadwick did: assessing your values, setting goals, and concentrating on outcomes.

Assessing Your Values

Assessing your values is an invaluable step towards achieving self-discipline. After all, how can you get where you're going if you don't know where you're going or why?

Ask yourself what you value. What drives you? What makes you pick the yard up religiously but keeps you from writing that children's book you've had in the back of your mind for the last decade? Consider the following values.

1. **Reputation.** How important is this and what would you do to create, maintain, or even repair a good reputation?
2. **Career success.** Success is important, but at what cost? How far will you go to become successful? Will you do anything? How do you define success? Do you include business, finance, and personal relationships in this definition?
3. **Honesty.** Think about your daily interactions and the part honesty plays in your dealings with yourself and others. Do you lie to others? Do you lie to yourself?
4. **Body weight and muscle tone.** Do you think it's important to be in great shape? Do you do something every day to be fit? It could be walking, running, or taking a bike ride. Have you gained weight and feel terrible about yourself? Are you doing anything about it?
5. **Personal attractiveness.** Is your attractiveness only physical or is it based on your personality and attitude? We've all met people who obviously aren't attractive but who have a magnetism that looks alone can't create. How far are you willing to go to become more attractive?

    In Maxwell Maltz's famous book, *Psycho-Cybernetics*, a plastic surgeon realizes that no matter how many nose jobs, face lifts, or tummy tucks he performs, many patients still don't see themselves as attractive. He discovers that personal image is not what you see; it's how you feel about yourself.
6. **Professionalism.** Do you work at being professional in your work and/or personal life? Professionalism isn't just being good at something; it also means growing and learning in your quest for improvement. Professionalism doesn't stop after your initial job orientation,

either. It continues as long as you want to be thought of as effective and valuable.

7. **Intelligence.** Do you have book smarts or street smarts? Combinations of the two make up intelligence. What will you do to gain intelligence? It's not simply a matter of formal study. There are lessons all around if we simply open our eyes and ears.

8. **Power.** There is personal power and position power. How hard will you work to achieve either? Many wealthy people care little about their income, but a lot about the status and power that money gives.

   Apparently the airlines haven't yet figured that out. With every new promotion they offer more free miles, but most passengers want first class upgrades and would freely give up miles to get better service.

9. **Money.** If there ever was a value that seems to drive people, it's money. How much does it mean to you? What are you willing to do to gain money and what does it mean when you make more of it?

   Best-selling author Michael Crichton, author of *The Andromeda Strain* and *Airframe*, was asked by talk show host Charlie Rose how much money he had. Predictably, Crichton said he didn't know and wouldn't say if he did. Rose pressed him and the author finally answered that money is a big deal if you don't have enough, but once you can pay your bills, it doesn't seem to matter very much.

10. **Status.** Do you care about your place on the social ladder or doesn't it matter all that much to you? What if you could use status to help others? Would that make a difference in the way you feel about it?

    I hate to admit this, but in 1998 I was eight thousand miles away from becoming a Delta Airlines 100,000-mile Platinum Status Flier. With this status level, I could upgrade for free and be assured of many perks a frequent flyer needs like free club room access at any

Assessing Your Values, Setting Goals, and Concentrating on Outcomes

major airport and an ability to board any airplane first, which allows me to always find room for my carry-on luggage. I rationalized that I couldn't fly my standard 8,000 miles a week if I had to endure the regular difficulties of airline travel, so I flew to Panama and New York within two weeks just to get the extra status. What are you willing to do?

11. **Honor.** Honor has often meant a great deal to soldiers throughout the course of human history, but how much does it mean to you? Will you work to gain the respect of others? Do you act on your values no matter what? When faced with a dishonorable act that no one will find out about, do you pick convenience or morality?

12. **Generosity.** People who are generous give not just of their possessions but of their time. Is this important to you? Think of the old song with the lyrics, "When you coming home, Dad?" to which the father replies, "I don't know when, but we'll get together then, ya, you know we'll have a good time then."

    Giving your time is a remarkably generous act. If you value it, do you give it?

13. **Ability to nurture.** Is taking care of somebody important to you? Some couples elect not to have children because they couldn't or choose not to take the time to nurture a child on a constant and ongoing basis. At the same time, many people act out a need to nurture with pets, treating them much as they would another human being. They hold conversations with their pets, play with them, even dress them up like little people. How great is your ability to nurture?

You can pinpoint your values by looking at how you behave every day. You can also examine your daily behavior to see where it strays from your values. Not only should your values take the highest priority in your life, the values you live by should direct, to a large extent, your behavior, thoughts, and activities. The following brief fable by Aesop illustrates this beautifully:

> Discouraged after an unsuccessful day of hunting, a hungry wolf came upon a well-fed mastiff. He could see that the dog was having a better time of it than he was and he inquired what the dog had to do to stay so well fed.
>
> "Very little," said the dog. "Just drive away beggars, guard the house, show fondness to the master, be submissive to the rest of the family, and I'm well-fed and warmly lodged."
>
> The wolf thought this over carefully. He risked his own life almost daily, had to stay out in the worst weather, and was never assured of his meals. He thought he would try another way of living.
>
> Then he saw a place around the dog's neck where the hair had worn thin. He asked what this was and the dog said it was nothing, "Just the place where my collar and chain rub."
>
> The wolf stopped short. "Chain?" he asked. "You mean you are not free to go where you choose?"
>
> "No," said the dog, "but what does that mean?"
>
> "Much," answered the wolf as he trotted off. "Much."

Once you have a handle on your values, you're ready for the next step—setting tangible goals you can achieve.

Setting Goals

Alan Kay once said, "The best way to predict the future is to invent it." If you know your values, you can set goals in accordance with the things you believe are important. The conflict and discomfort in reaching those goals will be minimized because what you're working for is what you really want, your heart's desire.

Slicing

The technique of slicing is a big help when setting goals. There are two ways to use slicing. "Slicing down" is a way to segment major concepts into smaller bits of information. For example, breaking the category "animal" into a smaller section might mean to slice it down into "marsupials" or "fowl" or even "rodents." Slicing down from the topic of "machine" might be to break the category into a smaller component like "plane" or "computer."

A "slice up" means the reverse, to expand something from a specific category into a broader one. To slice up "car" might mean expanding it to "transportation" or "trip." To slice up "anxiety" might mean to generalize into "psychological discomfort."

Slicing is important because it helps you organize your goals into a specific plan. I remember when I was in college that I wanted to earn both a Ph.D. and an M.D., but I became bogged down in just earning my doctorate. If I had known about slicing, I would have organized my life to earn my Ph.D. within three years; then I would have begun medical school. I would have worked backward, month by month, accomplishing what was needed in order to accomplish these goals.

Slicing is important because it helps you organize your goals into a specific plan.

You can use the concept of slicing to achieve more abstract goals, too. While the value of generosity sounds like something rather intangible, a developer named William Lyon has made it tangible enough to touch in the form of the Orangewood Children's Home in Orange County, California.

In fact, Lyon gives more than $250,000 a year to the Orangewood Children's Home, a refuge for molested and abused children.

Though he may not have thought of it this way, Lyon took the value of generosity and sliced it down to the tangible goal of giving away money. He then sliced his goal down into the very specific action of giving money to the Orangewood Children's Foundation.

Let's suppose a key value for you is attractiveness. If you were to slice that value down, it might be translated into the goal of becoming a beautician. In translating it even further, you might slice it down to enrolling in a two-year cosmetology program in which you'd learn how to design hair and various other beauty secrets.

I recall years ago that two of my very important values were fame and status. When I was fourteen, I went with a friend to a Herb Alpert concert at the San Diego Sports Arena. In the late 1960s Alpert's group, The Tijuana Brass, was among the most popular in the nation. When I stepped into the arena, I was shocked to see at least ten thousand fans packing the seats. As I sat there I became obsessed with the thought of one day being someone special. I never again wanted to be just an unrecognized face in the crowd. I wanted to walk into a huge group of people like that and have everyone recognize me, or at least be recognized as a VIP.

> *Your values stay with you and become part of your unconscious, directing much of what you do every day.*

It's interesting that, many years later, my goals of writing books and speaking around the world are likely the outcome of a desire to gain more recognition. You see, your values stay with you and become part of your unconscious, directing much of what you do every day.

This makes sense. Think about all the goals you once wanted to accomplish but didn't have the discipline to

Assessing Your Values, Setting Goals, and Concentrating on Outcomes

complete. Often, the reason you quit is that they didn't align with your values. They weren't important enough for you because you didn't believe in them enough.

I also remember years ago being pushed to play basketball because of my height. I wanted to make the team but didn't have the motivation to practice as hard as some of the other kids. Predictably, I was cut. Making the team wasn't valuable enough for me to make the sacrifices necessary to be a good player.

Likewise, it's kind of tough to discipline yourself to achieve better grades in college if you never had a desire to attend in the first place. It's equally tough to lose weight, no matter how many diet books you read, if a slim figure isn't really that important to you. And no matter how many times you tell others that you really want to spend more time with your family, if you don't place sufficient value on doing so, you won't organize your work life to achieve that goal.

By the same token, the way to approach a task you want to avoid is to see what completing it will do for your goals and values. For example, say there is a big report due that you really don't want to begin but one of your goals is to increase your family's financial health. At the same time, you value hard work and integrity in your business life. You decide to do a thorough job on the report, knowing that it meshes with your goals and values. Consciously reminding yourself of this makes it easier to do what needs to be done.

It's very hard to stay disciplined if your goals are in direct contrast with your values.

It also makes sense that, as many psychologists have suggested, it's very hard to stay disciplined if your goals are in direct contrast with your values. Goals are important, but values are their bedrock foundation. If the values underlying self-discipline are shaky, your goals will be as well.

A recent poll showed that fifty-two percent of all executives said if they'd known early in their careers that they'd be in their current jobs, they'd never have started that career in the first place.

My lawyer is one of these executives. He really doesn't like to practice law. He would have preferred to go into business as an entrepreneur, but now he's financially committed to raising a family of three boys. How disciplined do you think he will be trying to spend long hours building his practice? There is a lot of truth to the idea that you need to do something you love and the money will follow.

Assuming you're now ready to set goals, be smart about it. There are four key points to remember when setting goals and they are as follows:

Four Key Components of Setting Goals

1. **Be specific**. Think of tangible or specific goals you can work toward, such as "I want to complete my college education in five years" or "I want to be a top-level manager in my current company in five years." A desire "to be successful" is a common goal, but success is different for everyone. You need to think about what's most important to you, then find specific words and phrases to describe it.

    Likewise, use measurable criteria so that you can judge whether or not you've reached your goals, and don't worry if your goals seem big. There are no unrealistic goals, only unrealistic time frames. It may sound cliché, but it's better to plan something big and fall short than to set your sights too low.

2. **Schedule for short (in the near future), medium (in the next three to five years), and long-term (more than five years away) goals**. Often, having a long-term plan will help you develop a better sense of what your short-term and medium-term goals need to be. When I

consulted in the late 1970s with the New York Life Insurance Company, I asked a salesman for one goal that would motivate him. He said, "To be happy." I told him to write down three specific achievements that would make a contribution to his sense of happiness. He came up with a 560SEL Mercedes, $100,000 in liquid investments, and to be home at 5:00 P.M. daily so he could play with his kids.

3. **Be willing to sacrifice to achieve your objectives**. If your goal is to read a book each week, you're going to have to reduce activities in other areas. This might mean watching less TV, taking public transportation, or sleeping less at night. Can you do this? Are you willing to do this?

    My brother Kevin markets our sales and staff training videos to small and medium-sized businesses. He is a brilliant leader, often coaxing stellar performances out of mediocre people. One salesperson, Robert, was on his way to making more money than he had ever dreamed of. The problem was that Robert would go out on drinking and drug binges for days at a time. Kevin gave him warnings that Robert ignored and finally Kevin fired him. For two weeks Robert begged for his job back. Kevin felt sorry for the young guy and hired him again, but he also let Robert know that if this behavior occurred again, he would be gone.

    Within one month Robert again engaged in a drinking and drug binge and didn't come to work for three days. Kevin asked him why he was willing to give up a job he said he so desperately wanted. Robert admitted that he didn't have the discipline to say no to his friends when they wanted to go out. He then admitted he didn't have the discipline to say no later when he felt like getting high. The bottom line was, Robert wasn't willing to defer short-term pleasure for a greater pleasure later.

4. **Maintain self-discipline in your quest to achieve what you want.** As Henry Ford said, "Obstacles are those frightful things you see when you take your eyes off your goal." Without the discipline to put your dreams together, you only have aspirations that never become reality. One way to maintain self-discipline is to carry representations of your goals with you. For example, when I played pro tennis, one player confided that he carried a photo of the U.S. Open trophy in his wallet. Every morning he would take it out and stare at it as he ate breakfast. It helped him focus for the rest of the day.

You might set aside a few minutes every day to review such pictures to keep them constantly in mind. In this way you can take stock of your progress and make corrections to ensure that you're on target to meet your goals.

Concentrating on Outcomes

If a goal can be defined as an objective you wish to achieve by a certain date, an outcome is the goal you desire in even more specific terms. I once heard the difference between goals and outcomes defined by psychotherapist Jeannie LaBorde this way: Goals and objectives are like a pencil box that has been newly opened. Outcomes, on the other hand, are the same pencils sharpened and ready to use. Below is a five-step approach to creating outcomes for yourself:

FIVE-STEP APPROACH TO CREATING OUTCOMES

1. Focus yourself towards a tangible outcome or outcomes. Remember that outcomes are goals you can actually see, hear, and feel. While owning a new house

Assessing Your Values, Setting Goals, and Concentrating on Outcomes

is a goal, seeing that house with vaulted ceilings, a cherry wood kitchen, and a veranda overlooking the ocean is an outcome.

2. Be positive in how you plan for your outcomes.
3. Sense and perceive the way you will feel when you achieve your outcomes.
4. Make sure your outcomes fit neatly with the outcomes of those who are important to you.
5. Make sure your outcomes clearly incorporate short, medium, and long-term goals.

Let's look more closely at step one. For example, if your goal is to become rich, your outcome is to specify the amount of money that will make you wealthy. More specifically, if the goal is to make a six-figure income, the desired outcome might be to make an annual income of $101,500.

If your goal is to have a better family life, your outcome might be to spend at least one hour per day talking or interacting with your wife and kids.

If your goal is to become educated, the outcome might be to achieve an MBA within three years.

The second step in achieving outcomes is to be positive in the things you want. I heard one divorced parent say, "My goal is to make sure I keep my ex-husband from getting custody of my child." This isn't an ideal outcome, as this person may end up causing grief not only for herself but also for her child. A more positive outcome would be to say, "My goal is to make sure my child has a consistent and stable home life."

Another kind of positive outcome occurs when you work toward something that other people believe in. Take smoking as an example. Not only will other people be able to relate to your goal of quitting, they can encourage

> *Goals are simply things you'd like to accomplish, while outcomes give you a way to actually experience the goal before you strive to achieve it.*

you and help you to stay disciplined as you work toward your goal.

The third step in achieving outcomes is that you are able to perceive how you will feel when you have achieved your outcomes. Well-known researchers in language, neuro-processing, and psycholinguistics have discovered that people primarily think using one of three senses: sight, sound, and feeling. It's easy to apply this information to step three.

For example, if your goal is to be wealthy and your desired outcome is to make $101,500 in one single year, you might visualize $101,500 neat new green dollar bills in a paper bag stamped by the U.S. Treasury. Or, as you flip your fingers through these bills, you might hear the sound cards make as you shuffle them in a deck. Or, you might feel the slightly rough edges on these bills and note that the paper feels a bit more porous than the kind of writing paper you find in your notebook or textbook. In this way, you're able to see, hear, or feel what a desired outcome is like before you actually achieve it.

You cannot do this with goals. Goals are simply things you'd like to accomplish, while outcomes give you a way to actually experience the goal before you strive to achieve it.

The fourth step in achieving outcomes is to make sure your desires dovetail with the people you hold important in your life. I recently met a woman who wanted to spend money fixing up her house. Her husband's goal was to move into a new house. He didn't want to spend any more money on their existing home, so his wife's refurbishing goal was in direct conflict with his. If she had asked her husband more about his own desired outcomes, she might have discovered that he was interested in increasing the value of their home for later resale. If she had sold the refurbishing idea as a way to build resale value, they both might have been able to achieve their outcomes.

The fifth step in achieving outcomes is to create short, medium, and long-term goals and objectives. Let's use smoking again as an example. Suppose you want to stop smoking in three months. You might schedule a checkpoint for next week at which you will be down to three fewer cigarettes per day, while also setting a goal of how many cigarettes you will or will not be smoking at the end of the next several months.

Sculptor Francois-Auguste Rodin, when asked how he managed to make his remarkable statues, responded, "I choose a block of marble and chop off whatever I don't need." This might be a good approach. Whatever you do, don't copy the techniques used by the various law enforcement agencies in the following joke:

> The LAPD, the FBI, and the CIA were all trying to prove that they were the best at apprehending criminals. The President of the United States decided to give them a test. He released a rabbit into a forest and each organization was assigned to catch it.
>
> The CIA went in. They placed animal informants throughout the forest. They questioned all plant and mineral witnesses. After three months of extensive investigations, they concluded that rabbits did not exist.
>
> The FBI went in. After two weeks with no leads, they burned the forest, killing everything in it, including the rabbit, and they made no apologies. The rabbit had it coming.
>
> The LAPD went in. They came out two hours later with a badly beaten bear. The bear was yelling, "Okay! Okay! I'm a rabbit! I'm a rabbit!"

A couple of years ago I met a stressed mom who complained about all the work she had to do and the lack of time to do it in. She knew what she didn't want out of life but couldn't seem to think of what she did want. I asked her what she valued and of course she said her kids. I asked what her goals were for them and she had a list of things she wanted: to provide a good education for them, for them to be happy at home, for them to feel protected, for them to feel loved all the time.

I asked her to tell me how she would know if her kids were getting a good education. She said they would be on the honor roll at school. I then asked her how she could ensure their making the honor roll. She said if they diligently completed their homework every day, they would be able to get on the honor roll.

Puzzled, I asked her how that would help her feel less stressed. She said that most of her stress was with the kids after school. They fought and messed the house up while she was getting dinner together. I asked, "If they did their homework every day before watching TV, kept out of your way while you were making dinner, and didn't fight, would you feel less stressed?"

She smiled and said, "If you can do that, I'll be your friend for life."

I went one step further. I asked her to think about what her dream house would look and sound like at the end of the workday. She said, "It's all quiet. My kids are studying in their rooms. They pop in once in a while to ask me a homework question and say "Thanks, Mom" and go back to their work. I hear them talking to each other without bickering. I then ask them to come to dinner and they both tell me their homework is done." The woman was surprisingly detailed in her mind of what a blissful household looked, sounded, and felt like.

Uncovering this overworked mom's values and goals was the first step towards creating the outcomes she wanted in her life. While a lot of work remained for her to do, she was now on the right track to do it—and in fact *did* do it.

Like this woman, you too can assess your values, set goals, and concentrate on outcomes to achieve the self-discipline you need to make those values, goals, and outcomes come to life. This may be the stuff dreams are made of, but dreams can—with self-discipline—come true.

ASSIGNMENTS
Putting Self-Discipline to Work

1. Take another look at the list of values you read through earlier in this chapter. Now choose three things you particularly value, whether they're contained in this list or not, and write them down on a piece of paper in the order of their importance to you.

   Next, slice each of them down into a goal or goals. In turn, slice them down into actions you can take.

   For example, if one of your key values is to run your business more professionally, you may be able to make a couple of simple life adjustments. Perhaps you could take a few classes in running a small business or get to work earlier in the day in an effort to increase your income.

   Perhaps you wish to increase your stamina and physical fitness. You might slice this down into the decision to jog for twenty minutes each day at least five times a week.

2. Using the four key components of setting goals discussed in this chapter, write out at least two goals for yourself and how you'll begin to achieve them. For example, be specific, schedule for short, medium, and long-term goals, write down what you'll be willing to sacrifice in order to achieve your goals, and write down how you plan to maintain self-discipline as you work towards your goals.

3. Now use the five-step approach to creating outcomes for yourself by taking the two goals you identified in the previous assignment and following the five steps as you write out how you will identify and achieve these outcomes.

SECRET
three

Achieving Self-Discipline through Visualization and Recasting

> *A fool sees not the same tree that a wise man sees.*
>
> William Blake

There was once a little old man who fell into a pit. A banker came by and offered him a loan to pay rescue workers to get him out. A while later a psychologist came by and asked how he felt about being in there so long. After a few more hours, the man's friend saw him and jumped into the pit too.

The man screamed, "Why did you jump in here? Now we're both stuck!"

The friend replied, "There are two reasons I jumped in. One is that you are my friend and I wanted to support you. The second is, I know the way out."

The 1989 French Open tennis champion was the youngest winner ever. In fact, teenager Michael Chang nearly lost except for an extraordinary level of self-discipline. Part of what may have contributed to his success were the pictures he kept plastered on his bedroom walls for two years before he won the title—pictures of people winning a Grand Slam tournament. Chang not only had internalized this vision, he had also envisioned every point he'd play on the slow red clay courts of Roland Garros Stadium in Paris.

When he walked onto the court, he felt as if he'd been there before. He was so committed to fulfilling his envisioned destiny that at one point he served underhanded to Ivan Lendl. He was too tired to serve overhanded due to the pain of cramps, but even so he was able to win his serve. His vision of winning ignited the power that made his self-discipline come alive, and he fought off painful cramps to become one of the top ten players in the world.

Dr. Charles Garfield in his book *Peak Performers* reports that not only do athletes like Michael Chang understand the value of mental rehearsal, they've been doing it since long before psychologists discovered a name for it. He writes that everything from selling to speaking in front of a group to becoming a better golfer can be improved by practicing this technique of mental rehearsal, or visualization.

Visualization

When children decorate their bedroom walls with pictures and posters of people they admire, whether it's Superman, Wonder Woman, Teenage Mutant Ninja Turtles, or Michael

Jordan, they are using visualization. Vivid mental representations can give them the leverage they need to maintain self-direction. We adults can use the same technique to achieve the objectives we want.

In the sports world, images are what cause athletes to go from amateur to professional. Hall of Fame running back Walter Payton, in his heyday with the Chicago Bears football team, was once asked by a reporter how he was able to explode so quickly out of the backfield. Payton looked surprised at the question and said, "Why should it be so mysterious? I've run that pattern through the defensive line in my mind at least a thousand times. I've run it so often I knew exactly where the scrimmage line hole would be."

What is it about pictures—i.e., visualizations—that's so crucial to living a self-disciplined life? There are two factors that make pictures so effective in helping us maintain self-discipline. Factor one is that pictures allow us to focus on exactly what we're working for. Factor two is that it's difficult to make sacrifices and endure pain if we don't have a clear-cut image of what we're trying to achieve.

One of the reasons diets fall apart so quickly certainly has something to do with the dieter's hunger, but it also has a lot to do with the fact that the person on the diet isn't able to endure the discomfort of short-term hunger and exercise. This is because the discomfort causes the dieter to lose sight of what he's working for. If you're someone who has set a goal of losing weight, make sure you create a mental image of the way you would like to look. Turn that image into a big, bright, close, and colorful representation in your mind. Re-access that memory constantly to keep yourself on track.

> *It's difficult to make sacrifices and endure pain if we don't have a clear-cut image of what we're trying to achieve.*

Without a picture or mental photograph, we live from pleasure to pleasure, from moment to moment. I personally believe that one of the reasons so few people manage to maintain self-discipline and to accomplish great things in life is that they forget to draw out images in their minds of what they want to achieve. This lack of direction dooms them at times to lives of emptiness and at other times to lives of quiet hedonism in which they constantly move from one good feeling to the next. This may not sound terrible until you see a fifty-year-old who has spent his whole life searching for one good feeling after another and who now finds himself in a job and lifestyle he hates.

Develop Your Visual Side

Developing your visual side isn't tricky in the least. You can begin today by trying the following exercises.

Recasting

This mental technique, while deceptively simple, is used by superstars in all areas to reach short and long-term goals. You may not have heard of him before, but real estate developer Donald Bren is one of the ten richest people in America, as well as among the most wealthy in the world. Bren built his first house at age twenty-five with a $10,000 loan. He went on to become the single largest landowner in southern California, one of America's richest real estate markets.

How did he do it? Bren had a unique vision of the future. In 1983 he purchased prime southern California real estate. His goal was to develop it in his lifetime. In his office sat a model of each raw-land parcel, with buildings resting on them as if they were already developed.

Bren is past sixty-five now and close to seeing his scale model become life-sized, but he still arrives at work at 7:00 A.M., still pays attention to details, and even eats lunch at his desk.

Mental Substitution

To help further develop your visual side, try the technique of mental substitution: On a piece of paper write down the sign of a square root and put some numbers in it. Next to it write down an algebraic equation, one that you can remember. Now write down the symbols of multiplication signs, division signs, and other logarithmic or geometric signs. Concentrate on these symbols on your paper. Think about the emotion you feel as you look at them. If you're turned off, you're probably accessing the same experience you had in school when you were learning them.

Now take a minute and close your eyes. Think of a wonderful experience you had in the past, something that you were excited and motivated about, something that was enormously fun. It will be easy for you to access this experience if it happened to you recently. Now open your eyes and look back at the piece of paper with the mathematical symbols. Then close your eyes and go back and ponder the picture of the fun experience in your mind. Next go back to looking at the mathematical symbols. Now close your eyes again and return to the fun experience.

Now think of something emotionally very neutral, such as a road sign or a mountain. Then look back again at the equations. If you discover that your anxiety over these numerical symbols has decreased, you've just shown yourself that mental images can change your emotions.

Observation

Another way to gain more access to your visual side is to practice observing people. Right now, look at the person nearest you. This could be someone driving in a car, someone walking along the street, or someone lying around the pool. Look at that person for no more than three to four seconds. Now look away. Stop reading until you have done this.

Now verbally try to recall as many specific features about that person's looks as you possibly can. What color is their clothing? What color is their hair? How tall are they? Are they wearing glasses? How thin or heavy are they? Are they wearing tennis shoes, high heels, or flats?

This exercise not only helps develop your visual side, it's also extremely useful in helping you develop your memory.

Submodality Focus

I once asked a computer company executive who was competing directly with IBM and Hewlett Packard how his day had gone. He said, "Wonderful." He then told me about one of his scientists making a key component work more proficiently. As he discussed this he was extremely excited. I asked him if anything else had happened during the day and he told me about at least ten or twenty horrible things that had occurred. These included cash flow problems, staff shortages, and union negotiations. I then asked him what made the scientific benefit so wonderful. As he remembered, I noticed how elaborate he was in his description of the positive event and how non-descriptive he was of the more negative things that had happened during his day.

> *Submodality focus is the way we experience events.*

He was using a mental technique called submodality focus, which consists of the way individuals experience events. It's a key ingredient in maintaining self-discipline, and top business people employ it regularly to keep themselves positive.

Association/Disassociation

Another visualization technique that will serve you well is called association/disassociation. This is a way to separate

Achieving Self-Discipline through Visualization and Recasting

yourself from negative and limiting experiences that can wreak havoc with your discipline program.

Back in the early 1980s when I first started my consulting business, I met an interesting guy. Tom was a young entrepreneur in his mid-twenties, like I was. He was involved in the manufacture of fashion roller skates, one of the big fads in the early 1980s. Despite his enthusiasm, Tom went bankrupt in 1982. He was down but not out.

I recently saw Tom at a financial planning symposium. He is now a partner with a mutual fund company. While we had a cup of coffee, he described his distressing experience. He told me that he had been under financed and ill prepared. He hadn't known how to deal with cash flow problems or employees.

Incredibly, as Tom talked, he described his experience in the third person. He spoke of himself and his business as, "Tom had a tough time. The man who loaned Tom money didn't agree with the way Tom was running his business. Unfortunately, Tom got sick and tired of dealing with this person. He and Tom had a parting of the ways."

It was incredible to hear someone talk about himself this way. I don't tell someone a story and use the word "Kerry" in it; I use "I." But disassociating himself was Tom's way of separating himself from the negative experience. It was almost like he was watching a movie or a television show of himself having a bad experience.

On the other hand, as he told me about his current success, he used the word "I" constantly, as in *"I'm* successful now," "*I'm* making a six-figure income," "*I'm* now a partner with a large financial firm with the best products in the industry." Indeed, Tom truly was successful.

It probably should make sense to all of us that the more we relive events in our lives, the greater effect they'll have over our current and future emotions. If instead we vividly remember successful experiences and deliberately distance ourselves from bad ones, we'll be encouraged—and much more motivated—to risk and try again.

Attachment

One of the offspring of the association/disassociation technique is called attachment, which comes from a concept called psychological conditioning. Attachment is a way of changing negative experiences into positive ones. For example, have you ever run into a stranger who wore the same fragrance as that of a loved one? It might be the scent of your mother, wife, husband, or lover. When you got a whiff of that scent, you instantly thought of that person and possibly an experience with them.

This can happen with songs, colors, touch, lots of things, and you can put it to work for you. Recall a wonderful experience, a time when you did something great with family or friends. Access that experience right now. For the time being, make it extremely bright, colorful, and close. If you can hear the laughter and feel the smile that was on your face, so much the better. At the moment when you feel the highest level of enjoyment, touch yourself on your arm or hip or some easily accessible place. Then go back and relive the wonderful experience again, several more times.

The more we relive events in our lives, the greater effect they'll have over our current and future emotions.

This is a stimulus-response technique, similar to Pavlov's dog salivating in response to the smell of meat. Stimulus-response is one of the most powerful reactions in modern-day psychology. It's also one of the simplest techniques to use. Whenever you feel yourself becoming stressed, touch yourself in the same place. If you've successfully attached the positive experience to that touch, you'll be amazed at what happens.

Likewise, use attachment when you want to mentally plan for success the way Michael Chang did. First, breathe deeply until you relax. Let your mind wander, not concentrating on any one thing. Then start imagining what it is you want to achieve, such as giving a great speech or closing the biggest sale of your life. As you think of the success you would like to achieve, touch yourself in the programmed place. Do this a few times and notice the visualization of the great success come back simply by touching yourself. This is almost like a switch turning on a light, but in this case the light is an image that is full of success and power for you.

Attachment is a way of changing negative experiences into positive ones.

A key to making mental rehearsal work is to make the experience as real as possible and to use as many senses as you can think of. What does a win taste like? What does it sound, feel, smell, or look like?

Golfer Phil Michelson won the 1996 Phoenix Open with an incredible, once-in-a-lifetime shot. He was behind a tree on the thirteenth hole and had to make par to stay in the hunt. Fat chance. A great shot from that position might get him back on the fairway saving a bogey, but little else. He looked at the green and tried to remember what it had felt like the last time he'd hit an extreme draw from behind a tree.

A draw in golf is virtually a controlled hook, yet the word "control" is generous. This is one of the hardest shots in golf to hit, let alone land in the same fairway you are aiming for. Michelson lined up the draw and, to the gallery's amazement, curved the banana-shaped shot an astonishing 130 yards onto the green with a pitching wedge. The crowd went wild. When Michelson was asked by a reporter how he was able to hit such a difficult pitch, he said that he didn't do anything special. He simply remembered what it had felt like the last time he'd hit a draw from behind a tree.

When you remember a successful situation, it likely is in a different mode than you remember anxiety or failure. One mortgage loan broker mentioned that he remembers his best sale as a mental image and experiences sales anxiety as a voice in his mind. When I told him to *see* the next appointment instead of *hear* it, his anxiety and worry disappeared.

Like most motivational philosophers, Saul Miller believes that if you *see* yourself winning, you will be that much closer to doing it. If you *see* yourself doing it, you *can* improve your sales, management, sports, or any other performance.

In fact, you can experience future success mentally right now. Picture yourself not losing your temper with your three-year-old when he steals a toy from the baby. Instead, see yourself calmly, rationally, and effectively handling the situation. Or see yourself drinking a diet shake for breakfast and lunch instead of breaking down and having a hamburger. You might even visualize yourself craving a hamburger but then possessing the discipline to avoid the temptation and drinking that diet shake instead.

Recasting

In addition to using visualization, you can experience future success mentally by recasting your perception of what self-discipline is. Recasting works much like a frame around a picture. A poor frame can make any painting worse, just as a beautiful frame can make even a mediocre painting look substantially better. In some cases, the frame can look better than the picture itself. Recasting is built on the concept that there are no good or bad events in your life; there's only your perception of these events.

Recasting is not exactly visualization. It is more a rethinking or restructuring how you think about a concept or idea.

For example, if you decide to go into work at 7:00 A.M., your first inclination might be to think, "I will feel tired." To recast that idea might be to think, "If I go into work at 7:00 A.M., I will be able to get an extra two hours of work done without interruption. This in turn will help me to achieve my goals more effectively."

The key to recasting is to associate positive experiences with your goals and objectives.

I once developed a friendship with an airline pilot. His emotional picture frame was his career path of flying. He connected everything he thought of to flying or something related to it. If he saw a news report about Paris, France, he'd talk about a recent trip there. If we discussed food, he'd bring up airline cuisine.

Most people don't structure their thoughts to that extent, but we all see life in a way that limits or empowers us. While my friend was limited in his frame, it certainly served his objective of being a successful pilot. The way he framed the world made even the drudgery of his work enjoyable because he saw the entire world as if it were made for flying.

You can use this concept of recasting in developing a self-disciplined life. The key to recasting is to associate positive experiences with your goals and objectives and to disregard the factors in these experiences that seem to be obstacles, or at least to see them as opportunities to learn and cope. If you can do this, you'll have much more control over your life.

Context and Content Recasting

Two types of recasting that will change your attitude toward the negative aspects of self-discipline are context and content recasting.

Context Recasting

Context recasting refers to your ability to take a negative situation and make it positive in another context.

For example, say your flight is delayed four hours due to weather. You could become irritated, as most passengers do, or you could get four hours of work done without interruption. I was recently stuck in Newark, New Jersey, America's most delayed airport. Passengers were irate when a United Airlines flight was cancelled. Instead of becoming angry, I picked out a chair next to a power plug and started to work on this book. I was actually pretty happy that I had time to get some work done. But in fact, a recent BizTravel news report showed that only fifteen percent of travelers take the time that's available to work or get things done while they travel. Most sleep or simply stare into space.

I have written four books on airplanes. This could not have been accomplished if all my flights had been on time, and it could not have been accomplished if I hadn't taken advantage of the extra time that became available to me. Even so, recasting is more than making lemons into lemonade. It is thinking of your experiences as challenges and turning them into benefits.

Kobe Bryant of the LA Lakers is an orthodontics patient of one of my best friends. Kobe was born with a slightly recessed chin. My orthodontist friend offered to put braces on Kobe in an effort to bring forward the chin. Jaw surgery also would have been required. Kobe's only comment when presented with the elective surgery was to ask if it could help him shoot basketballs better. That kind of mindset is context recasting and has helped Kobe become one of the best and highest paid athletes in the world.

Achieving Self-Discipline through Visualization and Recasting

Take another example. Once upon a time, the 3M Corporation had trouble with the durability of one of their adhesive products. The company's goal was to sell more of it, but the durability problem made for a dwindling market. Though the adhesive was not effective at bonding materials permanently, it did adhere temporarily. One researcher used the concept of recasting and put just a little bit of adhesive on the back of a piece of paper to make it stick to nearly any surface. Was there an application this adhesive could be used for? You guessed it—Post-It® Notes were born.

The mule in the following story also used context recasting:

> There once was a farmer who owned an old mule. The mule fell into the farmer's well. The farmer heard the mule braying but after assessing the situation, he decided that neither the mule nor the well was worth the trouble of saving. Instead, he called his neighbors together and told them what had happened and enlisted them to help him haul dirt to bury the old mule in the well and put him out of his misery.
>
> Initially, the old mule was hysterical! But as the farmer and his neighbors continued shoveling and the dirt hit his back, a thought struck him. It suddenly dawned on him that every time a shovel load of dirt landed on his back, he would shake it off and step up! This he did, over and over again. Shake it off and step up . . . Shake it off and step up . . . Shake it off and step up . . .
>
> No matter how distressing the situation seemed, the old mule fought panic and just kept right on shaking it off and stepping up.
>
> It wasn't long before the old mule, battered and exhausted, stepped triumphantly over the wall of that well! What seemed like would bury him had actually blessed him, all because of the manner in which he handled his adversity.

Content Recasting

The second type of recasting, content recasting, is the mental act of changing what an event means to you. For example, a Christian looks at death not as the end of life but as a new beginning in the kingdom of heaven.

For a more down-to-earth example, take an entrepreneur who recently went bankrupt selling commodities in Chicago. He now has a successful business that consists of several busy hot dog shops. He describes his first business failure as getting an intense education in running a business.

> *Content recasting is the mental act of changing what an event means to you.*

Think of a project you've been putting off. Maybe it's something like repairing a piece of furniture. You can choose to see the job as taking away from the time you'd otherwise spend watching sports on TV, or you can choose to see yourself working on the repair and listening to the game on the radio and enjoying the experience more than you would had you actually been watching TV.

This technique works; you simply have to change the negative image of working on the furniture to one where you're having fun. You can even make the background of the new image in your favorite color and repaint it to include your whole family helping and telling jokes. If you do this, your attitude toward the dreaded experience *will* change.

If this technique seems unbelievably simplistic, think of the last time you did the gardening or another household chore you'd been putting off. Didn't you avoid it for a long time only to feel after you'd done it that the experience wasn't so bad after all?

My friend, sports commentator Terry Bradshaw, was a famous quarterback and tried his hand as a motivational speaker. He took what he learned from the field and speaking stage to the TV sports desk and recast his attitude and image in a positive way that empowered him to achieve his goals. He knew he wasn't as articulate as basketball great John Wooden nor did he have the speaking flair of Fran Tarkenton or even the attention to detail like Joe Thiesman, but he did have a huge amount of enthusiasm. So he worked on developing a flair for enthusiastic delivery in a way that every audience would find contagious.

The difference between recasting and just being positive is the permanence with which the new thought lasts. If you replace old negative memories with new positive perspectives, you will be able to keep past events from limiting your future success.

Recasting Emotions, Behaviors, and Memories

It is even possible to recast emotions, behaviors, and memories. This technique is based on understanding the neuro-linguistic programming (NLP) system first communicated by researchers John Grinder and Richard Bandler. The theory goes that your unconscious controls how you experience and perceive past memories and current events. It consequently controls all sorts of habitual behaviors, which frees you to think about more important and urgent things. For instance, you don't consciously think about braking your car when you come to a stop sign, but you break nonetheless. That you unconsciously do so frees you to think consciously about the scenery, people, or conversations about you.

If you replace old negative memories with new positive perspectives, you will be able to keep past events from limiting your future success.

However, such unconscious habits may not always be good for you. In some cases, as when you try to diet, they may in fact sabotage your self-discipline. I spoke to a woman a couple of years ago who had enormous trouble losing weight. She had tried every diet she could think of and nothing had worked. After several conversations, I learned that she had been raped as a teenager. She still struggled with that memory as well as with the poor self-image she'd had ever since. There was no reason for her to think of herself as unattractive, but her unconscious image of herself was hard to alter after twenty-five years. Thus, she found it impossible to lose weight, since her unconscious mind thought of herself as being unattractive. Her extra weight simply confirmed this. Being thin violated this idea, so she was unable to lose the weight.

> *We need to find ways to control our unconscious to get it to support our goals.*

The point is, like this woman, we need to find ways to control our unconscious to get it to support our goals. To do this we first need to know what our predominant thought mode is.

The NLP system mentioned above holds that people perceive the world in one of three different ways: in pictures, sounds, or feelings. Picture people make sense of the world by constructing or recalling images in their minds. If they can't make a mental picture of what you're saying, they may have trouble understanding your ideas.

Sound people make decisions largely on the basis of what they hear. They often talk to themselves in order to understand a message.

Feeling people tend to react viscerally. They get a gut emotion talking to you. They may feel hot or cold about you or an idea after just a few minutes of interaction. Many people call this intuition.

If you knew what system you were using to perceive, could you be more self-disciplined? You bet. The following approach focuses on your unconscious thought mode to help you recast your emotions, behaviors, and memories so they are more supportive of your goal to be self-disciplined.

Four-Step Approach to Recasting Emotions, Behaviors, and Memories

1. **Identify the pattern of behavior or thought you would like to change.** For example, many athletes like to think of their playing in visual terms. Many of my tennis player friends tell me they pick a place on the court to serve to and then imagine that image in their minds as they hit the ball.

   If you were to try to train them to hit a serve differently, you might give them a different image of the spin the ball had instead of actually physically training them to hit the ball differently. For example, a slice serve in tennis is hit by glancing the racket off the side of the ball. If you are a visual person, you would try to picture the tennis ball being peeled like an orange. You might also imagine the ball jumping straight up as it lands. This would give you a powerful mental image to use in order to achieve the goal of learning to hit a serve differently, as well as the change in technique to accomplish it.

   In 1977, I was in the middle of a struggle playing a professional tournament in Linz, Austria. I had only been competing on clay courts for a few months and still had trouble moving on this unstable surface. One of the problems was that my serves didn't have the same kick and speed they had on hard surfaces. The clay surface caught the ball and slowed it down. The harder I tried to hit the ball, the more faults I made. I lost five games in a row and became desperate.

   I had just finished reading a book by Tim Galwey entitled *The Inner Game of Tennis*. Galwey was the Zen-master of tennis. His teaching method was to focus not on how you hit the ball but on the result. This technique was totally different from any teaching method up to that time. I was desperate and ready for anything. After all, I was quickly losing the match.

I picked out a pebble on the clay surface where I wanted my serve to land and just let it rip. My ball landed within inches of the target and aced the German national champion who was my opponent that day. My next serve was a slice and jumped so high that it caught my opponent totally off guard.

The result was my service game immediately turned around and I won the match, all because I concentrated more on the result and goal than on the method to reach it. Methods are always important, but sometimes we get so stuck in technique that we paralyze ourselves.

2. **Use signals from your unconscious to determine the background reason for your unwanted behavior and to help change a habit pattern.** Most of our habitual behaviors and thoughts are unconscious anyway, so the way to go about this is to make your mind go blank and then pose a question to which you are looking for a "yes" or "no" answer. Separate the difference between the background reason for the behavior and the behavior itself. Again, do this by using unconscious signals that can be answered by "yes" and "no" questions.

3. **Identify a new, desirable behavior more in line with your goals.** Use your unconscious to help, using "yes" and "no" questions as a guideline.

4. **Determine whether the new behavior fits in with who you are without inner conflict.** Again use "yes" and "no" questions as a guideline.

For example, say the woman in our previous example who had been raped continued to consciously want to lose weight, even though her unconscious didn't support this goal. In step one, she would identify her eating habits as the behavior she wanted to change. Being thinner would be the goal she consciously committed to.

Achieving Self-Discipline through Visualization and Recasting

Step two in this process would be to get a signal from her unconscious about this goal. Again, the key to tapping into your unconscious is to think of questions with "yes" or "no" answers and then to pose these questions to your unconscious after first clearing your mind. The answers, negative or positive, won't come in a word but you will be able to understand them if you know what your predominant thought process is.

This is because some of the most common signals our unconscious sends us are based in our dominant thought mode. If your most powerful mode is using pictures, for example, be passively aware of signals like images in your mind. Are those images dark, light, or small? The way your unconscious may signal you is by changing those images. It may make an image smaller, signaling "no," or brighter, signaling "yes." Some people will even see a flashing "yes" in the mental picture as a response to a question.

If you want to lose weight, can you picture yourself as thin? Is the image pleasing? Is that image of a thin body bright and big, or dim and small? If it's dim and small, your unconscious may not be supportive of your weight loss program.

If your most powerful mode is auditory, beware of noises like ringing or other sounds that become louder in support of something, or quieter when there is opposition. Can you hear people telling you how thin you look? Or are the sounds ridiculing because you're too thin, as some think Calista Flockhart, of *Ally McBeal* fame, is?

If your most powerful mode is feeling, watch out for physical sensations. You might become aware that your fingers are tingling or your legs are warmer in response to the questions you ask. You also might get a feeling in your gut about the question you are posing. Do you feel warmly excited about being thin, or do you feel more dread as you contemplate the work it will take to lose weight? All of these signals are common, but you may feel others as well. Just remain aware of any signals your unconscious wants to use as you ask for "yes" or "no" answers to questions.

Tapping into your unconscious is essential when you're determining the background reason for the unwanted behavior. Ask your questions and then be alert for answers that come from the mode your body is reacting in. The woman in our example who wanted to lose weight discovered there was a secondary gain to being overweight—she received little attention from men. By asking herself questions, she determined that her unconscious resisted losing weight because being heavy saved her from the perceived pressure of dating.

> *Tapping into your unconscious is essential when you're determining the background reason for the unwanted behavior.*

To get your unconscious to stop protecting you through this secondary behavior, you need to acknowledge what it has been doing. Then you need to ask if there are other ways to protect yourself from the perceived threat besides the undesired behavior. Again, use a series of "yes" and "no" questions to learn what these alternatives might be.

In the case of the overweight woman, she might have asked her unconscious if she could protect herself from the pressures of dating by deciding not to go out with anyone for a certain period of time. Another question she could have asked was whether dating was really all that threatening. You see how it goes. Asking these questions occurs in a sort of stream-of-consciousness way in which one question leads to another.

Keep in mind, though, that from time to time all of us have secondary gains for not being able to stay self-disciplined. My tardiness in practicing the trumpet at age twelve grew out of my dislike of the instrument. I was consequently late to lessons and procrastinated practicing, but I was never late to baseball practice.

Likewise, procrastination in going back to college may lie in an unconscious desire not to leave your job as a waitress or bartender. Maybe you really like this job even though you don't make enough money at it. The truth is, you don't procrastinate doing the things you love. If you think you want the goal but are still procrastinating, you need to get your unconscious involved to find out why.

I once read a report about a pro golfer who, ten years before, was ranked in the top twenty in the world. He hadn't won a tournament in these ten intervening years and thought he also had the "yips," a tendency to hit the ball with a jerk without smooth control. It's sort of like trying to be extra careful around expensive china and then nervously breaking it all.

The interviewer asked some probing questions about his family and discovered the golf pro's spouse wasn't especially supportive. She wanted him to take a job as a local country club pro. He felt guilty about all the travel time away from his family and had trouble committing to his goal of a demanding practice routine to get back to the top twenty.

In step three of recasting emotions, you must create a new behavior in line with your goals. Again, let's use the example of the woman who wanted to lose weight. She found through her unconscious that she had a secondary gain of doing just the opposite. A solution for her was to change her goal of how much weight she would lose—say ten pounds instead of twenty-five. This way her behavior still changed, her goals were still met, and her unconscious had time to adjust to the new goal. Thus, she would be more readily able to support a further weight loss in the future if she so desired it.

In the final step of the four-step approach, you need to make sure the new behavior is in line with your unconscious goals. The woman who desired to lose weight tried to get a sense of the new discipline of losing weight in the context of, "Is this really what I want consciously and unconsciously?" As she checked her unconscious by using the "yes" and "no" questions, she also made a commitment to uncover new ways and techniques to take the weight off and keep it off. She then used the unconscious signals she had previously accessed to try to get her unconscious to embrace her goal of losing weight. Once she had done all these things, she was ready to work toward achieving her objective of becoming thinner, albeit a little at a time.

> Self-discipline can be like Aladdin's lamp—it can grant you just about anything you wish for.

When you use the techniques of visualization and recasting, self-discipline can be like Aladdin's lamp—it can grant you just about anything you wish for. All you have to do is know how to use the lamp. As the old saying goes, just beware what you wish for. You may get it!

ASSIGNMENTS
Putting Self-Discipline to Work

1. Do again the exercise that involves observing others. Look at a person and then look away. Describe to yourself verbally or in writing what that person looks like without looking back at him or her. Be as detailed as possible. Then compare your list with how that person actually looks and acts. As you practice this activity, your lists will improve and so will your ability to tap into your powers of visualization.
2. Think back on a pleasurable experience. See it in your mind. Notice the vividness of the images. Now turn up the intensity of the color, proximity, and brightness. Do you feel even happier and more excited?

Achieving Self-Discipline through Visualization and Recasting

    Then imagine a bad experience and see if you can turn down the vividness. Make your picture of this experience dimmer. See it off in the distance, black and white, dull and fuzzy. See if you can do this enough to reduce the emotional bad feelings you attach to this event. Does the different image cause you to think of the event as less important and less emotional?

3. Think of a goal you would like to work toward and, as applicable, use content and context recasting to help reshape your attitude toward achieving this goal.
4. Use the four-step process to recasting emotions, behaviors, and memories in committing yourself to working toward the goal you identified in the activity above.

SECRET **four**

Achieving Self-Discipline by Modeling and Using Mentors

> *I would never join a group that would have me.*
>
> Groucho Marx

Once upon a time, an elementary teacher named Mrs. Thompson stood in front of her fifth grade class on the first day of school and told the children a lie.

Like most teachers, she looked at her students and said that she loved them all the same. That was impossible, because there in the front row, slumped in his seat, was a little boy named Teddy Stoddard.

Mrs. Thompson had watched Teddy the year before and had noticed that he didn't play well with the other children, that his clothes were messy, and that he constantly needed a bath.

Willpower: The Secrets of Self-Discipline

This year, with Teddy in her class, Mrs. Thompson's dislike of him grew to the point where she would actually take delight in marking his papers with a broad red pen, making bold "X"'s and then putting a big "F" at the top of his papers.

At the school where Mrs. Thompson taught, she was required to review each child's past record. She put Teddy's off until last. However, when she reviewed his file, she was in for a surprise.

Teddy's first grade teacher wrote, "Teddy is a bright child with a ready laugh. He does his work neatly and has good manners...He is a joy to be around."

His second grade teacher wrote, "Teddy is an excellent student, well-liked by his classmates, but he is troubled because his mother has a terminal illness and life at home must be a struggle."

His third grade teacher wrote, "His mother's death has been hard on him. He tries to do his best but his father doesn't show much interest and his home life will soon affect him if some steps aren't taken."

Teddy's fourth grade teacher wrote, "Teddy is withdrawn and doesn't show much interest in school. He doesn't have many friends and sometimes sleeps in class."

By now, Mrs. Thompson was ashamed of herself. She felt even worse when her students brought her Christmas presents wrapped in beautiful ribbons and bright paper, except for Teddy. His present was clumsily wrapped in the heavy brown paper from a grocery bag.

Mrs. Thompson took pains to open it in the middle of the other presents. Some of the children started to laugh when she found a rhinestone bracelet with some of the stones missing and a bottle that was one quarter full of perfume. But she stifled the children's laughter when she exclaimed how pretty the bracelet was, putting it on, and dabbed some of the perfume on her wrist.

Teddy Stoddard stayed after school that day just long enough to say, "Mrs. Thompson, today you smelled just like my mom used to."

After the children left, Mrs. Thompson cried for at least an hour. On that very day, she quit teaching reading, writing, and arithmetic. Instead, she began to teach children.

Mrs. Thompson paid particular attention to Teddy. As she worked with him, his mind seemed to come alive. The more she encouraged him, the faster he responded. By the end of the year, Teddy had become one of the smartest children in the class. Despite her lie that she would love all the children the same, Teddy had become one of her special "pets."

A year later, Mrs. Thompson found a note under her door from Teddy, telling her that she was still the best teacher he'd ever had in his whole life. Six years went by before she got another note from Teddy. He wrote that he had finished high school third in his class and that she was still the best teacher he'd ever had in his whole life.

Four years after that, she got another letter saying that while things had been tough at times, he'd stayed in school and would soon graduate from college with the highest of honors. He assured Mrs. Thompson that she was still the best teacher he'd ever had in his whole life.

Four more years passed before another letter came. This time Teddy explained that after he'd earned his bachelor's degree, he'd decided to go a little further. The letter explained that she was still the best teacher he'd ever had, but now his name was a little longer. The letter was signed "Theodore F. Stoddard, M.D."

The story doesn't end there. Another letter arrived that spring. Teddy had met a girl and was going to be married. He explained that his father had died a couple of years before and he wondered if Mrs. Thompson might agree to sit in the place at the wedding that was usually reserved for the mother of the groom.

Of course, Mrs. Thompson did. And guess what? She wore that bracelet, the one with several rhinestones missing. And she made sure she was wearing the perfume that Teddy remembered his mother wearing on their last Christmas together.

As they hugged each other, Dr. Stoddard whispered in Mrs. Thompson's ear, "Thank you, Mrs. Thompson, for believing in me. Thank you so much for making me feel important and showing me that I could make a difference."

Mrs. Thompson, with tears in her eyes, whispered back, "Teddy, you have it all wrong. You were the one who taught me that I could make a difference. I didn't know how to teach until I met you."

ANONYMOUS

Human beings have an extraordinary capacity to motivate one another. The story of Teddy Stoddard shows that we can motivate for good, for ill, and for everything in between. Because of this, numerous individuals, famous and otherwise, have deliberately used the successes of others to maintain self-discipline.

The great military legend General George Patton spent much of his time during World War II reading about the exploits of Alexander the Great. In fact, Patton was so consumed by the legend of Alexander that he once believed himself to be the reincarnation of the great conqueror. He viewed Alexander's battles as historical events that would repeat themselves over and over again, and he thought that if he could mirror Alexander's character, he'd be much more effective in strategically planning his own modern-day battles.

Tennis great Jimmy Connors was likewise influenced while growing up by Rod Lavor, another tennis legend. He watched Lavor hit forehands that skimmed across the net with the attention of a jaguar scrutinizing his prey. He observed every movement, listened to every word, and matched every characteristic.

Lisa Johnson isn't famous, but she also uses the successes of others to maintain self-discipline. Lisa is an alcoholic who attends Alcoholics Anonymous (AA). There, a sort of buddy system is used in an effort to keep members accountable, since AA knows that having a partner to help mentor new members greatly increases the success rate of those trying to quit drinking.

For each of these individuals, the techniques of modeling and using mentors allowed the needed self-discipline to occur. You can use these techniques, too.

Modeling

As a youngster, did you ever put together a toy model of a ship, car, or plane by looking at the picture on the box? Did you ever dress or style your hair like your favorite hero, singer, or movie star? Have you ever started a new job and followed someone around for a few days or weeks to "learn the ropes"? Did you ever watch your mom peel a potato and then try it yourself?

Think of how you learned to play baseball . . . football . . . pool . . . Think of how you learned to swim, fish, or shave your legs or face.

Modeling what others do is a natural part of growing up. Anthropologist and comparative psychologist Conrad Lorenz demonstrated that all animals and human beings model for survival. Raising ducks from hatchlings, he discovered that motherless ducklings modeled him when they didn't have a mother duck to teach them duck behavior. When Lorenz walked, the little ducklings followed. When he went swimming, he had several little partners. When he dove underwater, guess where his swimmates were? Because of their instinctive drive to model, Lorenz was able to teach these ducklings to do things other ducks couldn't, such as sit at the dinner table and run in place.

We all need mentors, not only to learn new skills but also to model the most effective and efficient ways to perform them. To practice modeling, take a moment as soon as you can to ask someone how they do something. This could be anything from operating a computer to making a pie crust. Don't take "I don't know" for an answer. Most people know; they just haven't thought about the skill enough to put it into words. Help them by asking questions, and don't let them pass over any steps.

> *Don't worry if it seems like you're copying someone else's style. You'll eventually turn it into your own style.*

You'll have to pay close attention, because many of the skills and techniques we use are unconscious. This is why we can't learn a skill just by reading a book. We actually have to see the skill performed while it is described and then try it ourselves. If you've ever taken directions on how to get somewhere and later found the directions were incomplete, you know what I mean.

So take notes, even if it's a simple activity. After you listen to what your model says, try to perform the activity in exactly the same way your model did. Don't worry if it seems like you're copying someone else's style. You'll eventually turn it into your own style, and you can always improve on what someone else is doing.

I once asked my secretary how she was able to make the office copier work so well when it seemed to jam every time I used it. At first she said she didn't know, but when I pushed for an answer she said she first looked to see that the paper tracks were clear before she started. I watched as she put the paper in, nudging the door as she pushed the start button.

I took notes and did everything the way she did. After I began to model her actions, the machine jammed only once, and that was because I forgot one of her steps. By modeling my secretary, I saved myself days, if not weeks, of reading instructions from those complicated user manuals.

Years ago when I was getting started in the speaking business, I decided to model Mark Victor Hansen. He is now the editor of the phenomenally successful *Chicken Soup for the Soul* series. A gifted speaker, Mark has always used humor every two to three minutes in his presentations. He also uses verbal patterns such as, "What you impress in the recesses of your mind you can express in the reality of your world."

It sounds good, but I must admit, I didn't always understand a lot of it. Mark's style of speaking was masterful, but I knew his content wouldn't make sense coming out of my mouth. I soon decided I couldn't compete with the great speakers of the day in presenting motivational information, but I could compete on speaking about tangible skills that could allow listeners to increase their performance. I was able to successfully use stories and humor every couple of minutes to keep groups attentive, just like Mark did, and today my business has grown past most other speakers. I now speak in many countries around the world. I have even started a training company in sales and marketing and own a publishing company as well.

I modeled Mark Victor Hansen's style, yet I didn't copy him.

A couple of years ago, I watched a TV program about football quarterbacks. The reporter interviewed Dan Fouts, the great San Diego Charger's quarterback, now a TV sports commentator. In his ten years with the Chargers, Dan set passing records not only for his team but also for the rest of the NFL. Fouts was successful because he knew how to throw a timing pass. The reporter was trying to learn how Fouts did it. The reporter asked Dan what he thought about as he threw the pass. Fouts said, "I go back in the pocket to pass, then I make a picture of the pass pattern inside my head. I throw the ball to the 'X' in my mental map. If the receiver's there, he catches it. If he's not, someone else catches it. That about says it all."

The reporter, a little shocked at the simplicity, tried it. He missed a couple of times but after a few minutes' practice, threw the ball to exactly where the pattern placed the receiver. Fouts had spent years of self-disciplined effort in learning how to pass so well. The reporter needed a little practice, but the big shortcut he took was that he modeled someone else who was extremely successful. He went through each of the steps we've already covered in doing just that.

But learning a skill isn't all that's needed. You must also learn the thought process your model uses in perfecting that skill. I once asked a woman who had lost thirty pounds how she successfully stayed on her diet. She said she constantly saw herself as a young, svelte Christie Brinkley. When she was tempted to consume more calories than were allowed by her program, she would envision Christie's figure and pass on the chocolate.

You can also use the three thought processes of sight, sound, and feeling mentioned in Chapter Three to help you model. If you're a sight-based person, you can probably model simply by watching somebody do something. If you're sound based, you might have to say out loud each movement as you see it. Those who are feeling based need to know how it feels to do a certain task. Karate, for example, is easier learned for many people if they actually copy rather than merely watch the movements being practiced.

> *You must also learn the thought process your model uses in perfecting that skill.*

Most people do have to actually perform a task or action to fully internalize how to do it. This is a key difference between modeling something as opposed to simply learning it. In learning, someone teaches you the steps. In modeling, you learn the steps by reaching inside your model's mind

Achieving Self-Discipline by Modeling and Using Mentors

and going through the steps yourself the way your model goes through them.

For example, has anybody ever taught you how to shoot a bow and arrow? If so, they probably said, "Pull the string back and make sure the point of the arrow hits the bull's eye." End of story?

Not if you're a modeler. Instead, you'd say, "I understand how to do that, but what do you think about as you pull the string back? What do you see in your mind before you release the string? Do you hear the wind and adjust for distance? Do you feel the tension of the string and estimate how long you should hold it before you actually release the arrow?"

This is what you must do to successfully model someone. Don't just learn; model their internal experiences. If you do this, you'll develop results in a fraction of the time it would take someone else.

Modeling techniques have even been used by the U.S. Army. Their sharpshooters are the best in the world, but they possess special mental mechanisms that can't be learned by observation alone. Those who wish to perfect those same skills need to experience the same mental process the sharpshooters use. For example, psychological researchers have learned that sharpshooters breathe out just as they pull the trigger. This relaxes the body, while a breath in tenses it. By modeling that behavior, many others are able to duplicate the same success as the sharpshooters.

You can even model someone you've never come into contact with.

You can even model someone you've never come into contact with. This is tougher than working with a face-to-face model, but it can work. Use biographies and other writings to get inside the heads of successful people you'd like to model whom you'll never meet. Take Winston Churchill. With research, you're sure to learn not only about his administrative techniques but also about his ethics and values and even about his self-discipline.

One of the most disciplined people in history, Churchill was the perfect leader for England during World War II. He spent weeks in his bunker under a library outside of London, poring through territorial maps plastered on the walls, sleeping only about four hours a night. He worked with such discipline and intensity that generals and admirals rarely questioned his grasp of strategy. As long as he had a cigar, he was willing to work and fight forever.

Mentors

A mentor is someone you admire who agrees to help you achieve your goal, or at least a certain part of your goal. Using a mentor is a longer-term approach to modeling. Use the following seven steps to do it.

Seven Steps to Finding a Mentor

1. **Approach people who have done, or already are doing, what you want to do.** If finishing massive reports on time is your goal and there's someone in the office who continually does so, select that person.

    If you're in college and need help outlining and sticking with a specific career track, choose someone who's done this successfully.

    If your goal is to be a company manager, maybe you'll select a mid-level manager in your company who's on the way up. Maybe it will be a retired executive you've admired from afar.

    Many of these people were probably helped in much the same way by others and would probably be happy to help you, provided you come to them with respect for their time and a specific list of your needs. Emphasize that your main interest is in self-discipline. You want to know how they kept going through thick and thin and even sustained themselves through discomfort.

The mentor you choose should be substantially more successful than you presently are, though it is often tempting to stick with a mediocre mentor because they are more accessible than the great ones.

If you're not sure whom to choose as a mentor, try to think first of what you want to achieve in the end. Then work backwards, taking the first step in gaining the help of somebody who'd be willing to direct you. For example, if your goal is to become an international banker and you realize that accounting is a key ingredient in that success, try to get a mentor to help you learn about accounting. If your goal is to be a superb high school history teacher, think about the teachers you've had in the past who were effective as well as the teachers you work with now. Is there someone you greatly respect whom you could contact?

2. **Select mentors whose beliefs are similar to yours.** If your goal is to rise to the level of top executive in a firm while maintaining integrity and ethics, then it wouldn't do you much good to hook up with a "win-at-all-cost" mentor. There'd be conflict from the start.

After all, not all mentors teach positive lessons. Say your goal is to be a good parent. The following story makes it clear that, wisely or not, we parents are mentors to the children in our lives and are teaching them lessons every day, lessons that stay with them:

A frail old man went to live with his son, daughter-in-law, and four-year-old grandson. The old man's hands trembled, his eyesight was blurred, and his step faltered. The family ate together at the table, but the elderly grandfather's shaky hands and failing sight made eating difficult. Peas rolled off his spoon and food rained onto the floor. When he grasped a glass with his shaking hands, he spilled milk on the tablecloth.

The son and daughter-in-law became irritated with the constant mess, so they set a small table in the corner. There Grandfather ate alone, while the rest of the family enjoyed dinner together. Since Grandfather had dropped and broken a dish or two, his food was served in a wooden bowl. When the family glanced in Grandfather's direction, sometimes he had a tear in his eye. Still, the only words the couple had for him were sharp admonitions when he dropped a fork or spilled food.

The four-year-old watched it all in silence.

One afternoon, the father noticed his son playing with wood scraps on the floor. He asked the child sweetly, "What are you making?"

Just as sweetly the boy responded, "Oh, I am making a little bowl for you and Mama to eat your food in when I grow up." The four-year-old smiled and went back to work.

The words so struck the parents that they were speechless. Then tears started to stream down their cheeks. That evening, the husband took Grandfather's hand and gently led him back to the family table, where for the remainder of his days he ate every meal with the family. And, for some reason, neither the husband nor wife seemed to care any longer when a fork was dropped, milk was spilled, or the tablecloth was soiled.

ANONYMOUS

You can get some idea of a prospective mentor's beliefs before you even talk to him or her by listening to what the grapevine has to say. Even though it's probably not all true, it can still give you some interesting insights about how the mentor is perceived. Read articles or reports this person has authored. Look at the results of projects and programs this person has been instrumental in implementing. You can tell a lot about a person's beliefs by the causes with which they're associated.

> *If you find that your values and theirs don't mesh, back off and find a new mentor.*

If you find that your values and theirs don't mesh, back off and find a new mentor. Even if this person is extremely successful, you'll have an inner conflict following beliefs that are counter to your own, since it's essentially this person's beliefs that created his or her success.

Look at it this way: If you wanted to develop the discipline to start an employee appreciation program, think of how difficult it would be to develop that self-discipline with somebody who didn't think employee appreciation was a priority.

3. **Beware the all-talk, no-action mentor.** I remember in my early days as a speaker being very impressed by the bravado other speakers exhibited when they were talking about their abilities. They were very accessible, giving me advice on everything from how to attract clients to what to say during a presentation. But these people weren't any more successful than I was at the time.

Instead, what I needed was to find someone who was extremely successful, who had separated from the rest of the pack, who could help *me* separate from the rest of the pack.

4. **Try to choose a mentor who can be a life coach as well as a life teacher.** A teacher tells you how things are done while a coach has a vision of success and knows how to share the steps that are necessary for you to gain that vision. The best mentors are coaches

and more; they genuinely care about your goals and progress.

Green Bay Packer's coach Vince Lombardi was one of these people. He wasn't just a coach; he was a mentor. Thus, in addition to teaching blocking, passing, and running plays, Lombardi taught his philosophy about the game of football and the game of life.

My friend, football great Bart Starr, played quarterback for Lombardi. He told me he wouldn't be half the businessman he is today if it weren't for the philosophies Lombardi shared both on and off the field.

For example, Lombardi was famous for saying, "Winning is not the most important thing; it's the only thing." But Lombardi is much more famous for teaching discipline and deferring what you want now to reach a future goal later. He also stressed the importance of teamwork and being a contributing member of that team. These are lessons his former players have applied years after they've left the field.

That's because self-discipline and self-direction work, whether they concern football, fending for yourself in the business world, or taking care of your physical and mental well-being.

5. **Once you've selected a mentor, ask for his or her help.** You might put your request in writing, outlining a possible schedule for regular get-togethers, obligations of both sides, and your goal in utilizing your mentor's expertise. You need to be clear and concise. Emphasize that any arrangement would be at your mentor's convenience. If you waste a mentor's time before he or she even agrees to help you, you might be finished before you've begun. Be realistic and think about what you need and what you can expect your mentor to give, and be ready to accommodate your mentor's schedule and needs.

Be up-front at your initial meeting about why you want to see your mentor. You might even submit a list of written questions for the mentor to consider. Ask about your mentor's goals, attitudes, work approaches, and feelings about family, politics, or anything else you believe is important. Of course, you'll keep all this information confidential and you'll assure the prospective mentor of this condition.

Also be self-disciplined when you first attempt to contact your mentor. When I first started out, I contacted a speaker who was already famous in the real estate industry. In my initial meeting with Mike Ferry, he told me right away that becoming a speaker was the wrong thing to do. He then proceeded to tell me that he only had another five minutes before he needed to go. I was shocked and disappointed. I had wanted to develop my consulting career by speaking, but Mike took all the air out of my balloon.

I called Mike back after a week and asked to meet again. He told me no. I called a third time to meet and this time he said yes. At this meeting, he said that speaking was a great career but that he received so many calls from budding speakers that he had to find a way to filter out the ones who didn't have the perseverance to be successful. If I had not called him three times, you would not be reading this book today.

6. **After your mentor has agreed to work with you, emulate everything about him or her.** Even if you think some of your mentor's ideas and strategies are silly, give them a try and learn how they do them. If your mentor reads an industry magazine every night before he goes to bed, it's a good cue for you to do it too. If your mentor is trying to develop a new idea and does one hundred push-ups to foster his creativity, there must be a reason. Ask, and then try it yourself. If

a mentee were to ask me how I come up with my most creative ideas, I would say by taking showers. I take long showers in the morning and spend much of the time just thinking about new concepts. It may sound silly, but it works for me. Perhaps it could work for you, too.

7. **Regardless of your goal, be persistent in scheduling meetings with your mentor.** You must realize that if the mentor is good, you may be in competition with others who'd like to learn from the same person. Also be flexible: You may need to meet your mentor at the park for an early morning run and a cup of coffee afterward, even though you hate exercise and like to sleep in, because that's when it's convenient for your mentor.

See if you can meet with your mentor at least weekly to review your activities and problem solve, but realize that mentoring is a two-way street. Remember the movie *The Karate Kid*? The Japanese master was very interested in teaching the youngster Aikido. However, he made sure the young man gave something back while he was taking from the master. In one scene, the teacher had the youngster paint his house to learn Karate's up and down blocking motion. In another scene, the teenager learned a move through waxing the master's ancient car. Remember "Wax on, wax off"? Not only did the young man learn how to be more physically powerful by doing the exercises, he also learned how to give something back to the relationship as well as the psychological philosophies behind those lessons.

Meet with your mentor at least weekly to review your activities and problem solve.

What about losing weight? Can you use a mentor for this also? Easily. All you have to do is find someone who has lost the weight you want to lose and who has

Achieving Self-Discipline by Modeling and Using Mentors

been successful keeping it off. Talk to this person at least weekly about their eating habits and what kinds of exercises they do to maintain the discipline you desire for yourself.

One mentor of mind was the late Joe Charbonneau. Joe was a rotund man and a gifted speaker who lost over one hundred pounds in three months, but the real story is what he taught me about developing a video training business.

The biggest problem for any speaker is what to do when business dries up in December and August of each year. Thanks to summer vacations and the holidays, those are starvation months for speakers.

After watching me suffer too many of these down periods, Joe asked if I would like to gain enough income to bolster the slow times. I thought he was trying to sell me a network marketing plan, but he was such a good friend I didn't dare do anything but listen.

Instead, Joe told me he'd developed a series of twelve video tape programs and had sold the whole series, one tape at a time, to the clients who booked him to speak. He explained the program to me for three hours and I couldn't believe its simplicity or how well he had developed it. All I had to do was film twelve video programs and then sell them to my clients like Joe. I also had to develop a billing system in order to keep track of the clients.

I tried the program and initially it worked wonderfully. Most of my clients were very keen on gaining more information they could implement over the long term. They all wanted to utilize my ideas and make money with what they learned. But within two weeks of selling the series, I learned a startling fact: I couldn't make money with Joe's video system because clients weren't paying their bills.

I called Joe and asked how many uncollectable deadbeats normally ordered videos but didn't pay. He confided that thirty percent paid late or not at all. He didn't have anyone to follow up, so the numbers kept climbing higher and higher.

My solution was simple. I asked for and received credit card numbers and billed the cards monthly for each new video series. This one modification was the difference between profit and failure. Later we even offered a free thirty-day trial only requiring the buyer to pay for the shipping costs. We also were able to get each buyer to sign a fax sheet indicating they'd agreed to the purchase. This helped immeasurably when they forgot what they had purchased and disputed charges.

The lesson I learned was that while we all need to have mentors, we have to make their ideas work for us. We can't merely adopt what they do and stop there. I was able to use eighty percent of what Joe taught me, but had I used all his ideas without improvement, his system would have been a bust.

Using models and mentors clearly works. At the same time, it should be equally clear that we *need* models and mentors. But as we go about the task of modeling others and finding mentors to help us achieve our goals, we would be wise to remember that we act as models and mentors every day to those around us. Let's choose and use this power prudently.

ASSIGNMENTS
Putting Self-Discipline to Work

1. Learn a new skill—anything from baking bread to learning to sail to changing a tire to learning to be a good manager—by modeling someone's actions. Pay close attention to everything your model does. What

are the steps your model takes? How does your model react to interruptions? What is your model thinking as he or she goes about a task or the day? Ask questions and emulate your model as closely as possible, both physically and mentally.
2. Write down one of your goals and list a number of people who might be good mentors to help you achieve it. Then go through the seven steps we've discussed for using a mentor. As you meet with your mentor, use the modeling techniques we've covered to help develop your self-discipline. Try to think of a way you can give back to your mentor as well, whether in future credit, current assistance, or personal gratitude.

SECRET

Achieving Self-Discipline by Changing Your Beliefs

When in doubt, duck.

Malcolm Forbes

During a momentous battle, a Japanese general decided to attack even though his army was greatly outnumbered. He was confident they would win, but his men were filled with doubt.

On the way to the battle, the army stopped at a religious shrine. After praying with his men, the general took out a coin and said, "I shall now toss this coin. If it is heads, we shall win. If it is tails, we shall lose. Destiny will now reveal itself."

He threw the coin into the air and all watched intently as it landed. It was heads. The soldiers were so overjoyed and filled with confidence that they vigorously attacked the enemy and were victorious.

After the battle, a lieutenant remarked to the general, "No one can change destiny."

"Quite right," the general replied as he showed the lieutenant the coin, which had heads on both sides.

A few years ago, a New Jersey family was returning home from out of state after visiting relatives. When they approached the state line, they were shocked by what they saw. On the turnpike was a sign that read, "The State of New Jersey is closed." To make matters worse, a policeman stood next to the sign, apparently enforcing the closure. As the mom and dad exited the car, they stared for a long time at the sign, wondering when the state would reopen. When they finally asked the trooper when they could enter, *Candid Camera* producer Alan Funt walked out, explaining that they were on TV.

Would you fight a difficult battle with the odds stacked against you?

You would if you believed you would win.

Would you fall for something as silly as your state being closed?

The answer is the same: You would if you believed, no matter how ridiculous it might seem upon reflection. As Julius Caesar said some two thousand-plus years ago, "Men willingly believe what they wish."

Unfortunately, some of us, like the parrot in the short joke below, believe when we shouldn't:

Once upon a time, a magician was working on a cruise ship in the Caribbean. The audience was different each week, so the magician allowed himself to do the same tricks over and over again.

There was only one problem: The captain's parrot saw the shows every week and began to understand what the magician did in every trick. Once he understood that, he started shouting in the middle of the show, "Look, it's not the same hat!" "Look, he's hiding the flowers under the table!" "Hey, why are all the cards the ace of spades?"

The magician was furious but was unable to do anything about the parrot; it belonged to the captain after all.

One day the ship had an accident and sank. The magician found himself on a piece of wood in the middle of the ocean with the parrot by his side. They stared at each other with hate but neither uttered a word. This went on for several days.

After a week the parrot finally said, "Okay, I give up. What'd you do with the boat?"

As this story makes clear, beliefs have nothing to do with reality. Instead, beliefs are the foundation of the saying, "Whether you think you can or you think you can't, you're right."

This is a good thing. It means we can change or alter our beliefs at any time to support the self-discipline required to meet our goals.

A short time ago I was touring the island nation of Singapore during the religious festival of Pusan. This is a Hindu celebration in which true believers give thanks and offer atonement for spiritual transgressions. During the ceremony I watched faithful believers from virtually every walk of life pierce their skin by putting long, slender rods in their mouths and then through their cheeks. The surprising fact

> *Beliefs have nothing to do with reality.*

was that not one of the hundreds who pierced themselves bled.

This is just one example of the force belief can have in our lives, a force that apparently even has control over bodily functions such as bleeding when wounded.

Think of what the rest of us could accomplish if we could harness our beliefs to this extent. If we had this kind of control, using self-discipline to achieve our goals would be a snap. It's the kind of belief the young boy on the Little League baseball team had: When asked by a latecomer to the game what the score was, the boy replied with a smile, "We're behind fourteen to nothing."

"Really," the latecomer said. "I have to say you don't look very discouraged."

"Discouraged?" the boy asked with a puzzled look on his face. "Why should we be discouraged? We haven't been up to bat yet."

Using Visualization to Change Your Beliefs

In Chapter Three, I discussed how visualizing success can affect our behavior. After all, images power our beliefs as well as the doubt that shakes them. Doubt exists when there's insufficient faith in a belief, but belief exists when there's a commitment to accepting something that may not always be provable.

But belief exists when there's a commitment to accepting something that may not always be provable.

To demonstrate how our minds represent a belief in doubt, call to mind one of your very strong beliefs. This belief might be religious, ethical, or even related to the way you do business. Try to get a visual image of that belief and what it's done for you in the past. You might recall something that you prayed for that came to pass or a situation in which ethics paid off for you.

Achieving Self-Discipline by Changing Your Beliefs

Perhaps it's your strong belief in the concept of freedom symbolized by the Statue of Liberty, or your belief that good things come to those who wait as symbolized by the image of your grandmother who, after struggling through the accidental death of the abusive man she'd married when she was only nineteen, met and married the loving, supportive man who became your grandfather.

Now try to picture something you doubt. This should be something that may or may not be true. You may not even be sure. You might think of extra-terrestrial beings and symbolize them in your mind with a picture of a flying saucer or you might think of your secret desire to be the head of your department at work and envision a large, sunny office with a cherry wood desk.

Now notice the visual differences in the pictures that represent your belief and your doubt. You probably see the belief picture as big, detailed, bright, and colorful, while the picture of what you doubt is probably much smaller, fuzzier, and maybe only in black and white. If you pay attention to your emotional and physical processes, you'll probably notice that when you visualize an important belief you breathe slowly and deeply. Your hands may get warmer as the blood flow increases in your body.

> *When you experience doubt, you become stressed.*

When you experience doubt, you become stressed. Your breathing will become more shallow and your hands possibly colder and more clammy. This is one of the reasons why people who believe in something are so much more courageous than those in doubt. Strong beliefs can make us brave to the point that we are even willing to give our lives. How else can the willingness of Islamic extremists to offer themselves as suicide bombers be explained?

The great thing about belief is that it's always a choice. We can choose beliefs that limit us or beliefs that create power in our lives.

Let's say you want to stop smoking but you've tried and been unsuccessful. Did you believe from the start that you could accomplish your goal? Did you actually open the door to success in your mind?

Think of the power you'd have to take on the goal of quitting smoking or losing weight or completing a report if you believed from the start that you could do it. All along you'd approach the goal from a position of success instead of doubt. That belief in your own ability would do wonders for your self-discipline.

Give it some thought. Then use the two following exercises to try to change the way you approach your goal, whatever it might be.

Identify Positive Traits

This technique asks you to list an outcome you'd like to achieve and under it to write all the things you know about yourself that will help turn this outcome into reality.

As you develop your list, think about whether you have the determination and drive to complete your task, especially if you remind yourself of these positive traits.

Chances are, you do. All you need is to strengthen your supportive internal belief and to forget about the things you think will hold you back. Reviewing this list every time you doubt your ability to finish the task will help shore up your belief in yourself and your ability to reach your goal.

Visualize Success

Review the positive traits you identified above and imagine yourself applying them to your outcome. Make a picture of each. Thoughts about these supportive actions should be large, bright, and vivid. Any negative thoughts should be dim, black, and small to reduce the effect of doubt.

Where Beliefs Come From

It's easier to use beliefs to our benefit if we understand where our beliefs come from. Beliefs don't develop because someone hits us on the head one day telling us what we can and can't believe. Rather, beliefs come from four very tangible sources: our surroundings, what we discover intellectually, our experiences, and our hopes and expectations.

1. Surroundings

You've no doubt discovered that childhood has a great effect on success later in life. As discussed in an earlier chapter, if you grew up in a lower middle-class neighborhood it might be hard for you to experience great wealth in your life due to an unconscious belief that just paying the bills is supposed to be a struggle. But if your name were DuPont, Rockefeller, or Rothchild, your expectations and beliefs would be quite different. You'd be uncomfortable worrying about paying bills because your parents never did.

Ask yourself, are the outcomes you desire consistent with the surroundings you experienced when you grew up? If they're not, can you cope with the differences in lifestyle these outcomes might bring? If you're a salesperson trying to make more money, do you believe you can cope with the changes greater wealth will bring? Do you believe you really want money and greater wealth?

You're probably answering an enthusiastic "Yes!" but be careful: If you don't really believe you can or should make a six-figure income, you'll unconsciously sabotage your self-discipline in your attempt to do so.

To see if your belief is compatible with your goal of making more money, employ the technique called future belief check.

Future Belief Check

In your mind, see a visual representation of a specific outcome you desire. Now see an image of yourself with that outcome to determine whether or not you think you deserve your outcome. How vivid can you make that picture? Is it bright? Is it large? Is it colorful? If it isn't, this outcome may not be consistent with your beliefs. You need to either change the outcome or change your belief.

2. Intellect

The second source of our beliefs is our intellect. Here's how to use your intellect to check your beliefs. Take the same outcome you used in the last example. See the picture in your mind and check it to see if you believe you're intelligent enough to achieve that outcome. If your outcome is to complete college, do you believe you're sharp enough to get good grades? Your friends may know that you are, but do you know it? Imagine yourself wearing a graduation gown or carrying an armload of books and check for the vividness, brightness, and size of the image.

3. Experiences

The third source of our beliefs are our experiences. If you've been successful achieving things in the past, you'll likely be successful in the future. But if you've experienced stumbling blocks or limitations in the past, you may find it difficult to change your expectations of what will happen in the future. However, it's not impossible. Let's try the belief check again. Imagine your outcome once more and next to it envision a past failure. Then try to see the outcome as completed, shored up by your experience of the past. Is that picture vivid, large, and well defined? Will your past experience give you the self-confidence you need to succeed in the future to achieve this specific outcome? The picture and its characteristics will give you a good idea of the answer.

4. Hopes and Expectations

The fourth source of our beliefs are our hopes and expectations of the future. Unless we hope very strongly for something, this is one of the hardest ways to develop strong beliefs. That's because there are so few tangible things other than faith on which to base future expectations. Even so, most of us probably have a belief right now that when we go to work tomorrow, we'll have a good day. Being able to develop the future belief that we'll be successful is the lifeblood of commissioned businesses like sales.

I like to think of the story of little Jamie Scott when I consider hopes and expectations. Jamie was trying out for a part in a school play and had his heart set on being in it but his mother feared he would not be chosen. After school on the day the parts were awarded, Jamie rushed up to his mom, his eyes shining with pride and excitement.

"Guess what, Mom!" he shouted. "I've been chosen to clap and cheer!"

A friend of mine is a classic example of someone whose beliefs come from her intellect and experiences though *not* from her surroundings or her hopes and expectations. Suzanne, a happy homemaker in her mid thirties, has been afraid of flying her entire life. The fact that airplanes are statistically safer than cars is meaningless to her. After all, planes do crash, though not often. It doesn't help matters that every news article she's ever seen on the subject has permanently imprinted on her brain, empowering her belief that crashes happen more often than in fact they do.

Suzanne is an intelligent woman. She actually uses her intellect to increase her fear of flying. "Are several tons of steel *supposed* to fly through the air?" she asks. She reasons that even if flying is generally quite safe, any flight *she* happens to be on will crash. She feels this way even though no one in her family entertains such fears and in spite of the fact that her parents and siblings enjoy flying.

Because of her fear of flying, Suzanne and her family exclusively take driving vacations, even though they can afford more luxurious trips. She's missed out on a few significant opportunities over the years—a trip to Aruba with friends after college graduation, the honeymoon in Greece her husband had wanted—but all in all life has gone pretty smoothly.

Now she's being forced to confront her fear thanks to a family wedding on the other side of the country that's scheduled back to back with her son's hockey tournament. She can't miss one or the other, and that means flying.

Her husband is relieved the issue is finally being addressed, but as the days before the trip pass by, Suzanne is becoming increasingly fearful. She's having trouble eating and sleeping and has lost weight. Plain and simple, she needs to change her beliefs.

Changing Our Beliefs

As in Suzanne's case, beliefs can be self-sabotaging, especially when the beliefs we hold are bad for us or when they are incorrect. It sometimes takes a problem or tragedy to illuminate our knowledge to the point that we can change. The following story illustrates this beautifully.

> A man once found the cocoon of a butterfly. He began keeping an eye on it and one day noticed that a small opening had appeared. The man sat and watched for

several hours as the butterfly struggled to force its body through the little hole. Then the butterfly seemed to stop making any progress. It appeared as though it had gotten as far as it could and could go to further.

The man decided to help the butterfly. He took a pair of scissors and snipped off the remaining bit of the cocoon. The butterfly then emerged easily, but it had a swollen body and small, shriveled wings.

The man continued to watch the butterfly because he expected that, at any moment, the wings would enlarge and expand to be able to support the body, which would contract in time.

Neither happened! In fact, the butterfly spent the rest of its life crawling around with a swollen body and shriveled wings. It never was able to fly.

In his kindness and haste, the man did not understand that the restricting cocoon and the struggle required for the butterfly to get through the tiny opening were nature's way of forcing fluid from the body of the butterfly into its wings so that it would be ready for flight once it achieved its freedom from the cocoon.

ANONYMOUS

Fortunately, sometimes with education and sometimes with self-discipline, we can change our beliefs to support our goals. One way of doing this is with what is called a sub-modality change technique that can help us discover how beliefs can be diffused and reformulated in a new way.

Sub-Modality Change Technique

To explain this technique, envision a belief you hold. Play with each pictorial difference that exists in this belief. Try to change those characteristics in brightness, color, vividness, size, and other differences that you may notice. Make sure the belief is very specific.

For example, make your belief about future wealth a big house in the countryside. Make your belief about becoming a better golfer a picture of you winning a major tournament in a couple of years. If your belief is that you will receive an advanced education, you might imagine a cap and gown in your mind. Use whatever represents your belief in the most visual and tangible way you can.

Now call up the belief that you want to change and alter the characteristics of that picture. If your belief is large, make your picture very small. If your belief is bright, make your picture very dim. If it's detailed, make your picture fuzzy. If your belief is stable and static, make your picture flash. If your belief has color, change it to black and white. With each of these steps, notice the psychological and emotional changes you undergo.

Next, deliberately weaken the belief you want to change. Once you make this picture dim, small, and in black and white, you'll start to see it flash as it fades away. If you leave that frame empty with no picture to replace the belief you want to change, you'll experience even more anxiety. Instead, replace it with a belief you do want to have: You have the power to lose as many pounds as you want. You have the ability to fire a staff person who is unproductive, late, and rude. You have the power to overcome your habit of not really listening to the people around you. Weaken the doubt image of yourself, eliminate it, and then replace it with the image of you practicing the needed self-discipline.

My friend Suzanne was able to do this. She knew she wanted to overcome her fear of flying. She began by envisioning the belief that she and her husband would have a wonderful time on the coast of Maine watching their niece being married and celebrating with her sister and brother-in-law and all the various relatives. She imagined the lobster boil on the eve of the wedding and made that picture bright, vivid, and large. She was so successful at conjuring up the experience of eating fresh New England clam chowder that her mouth watered.

Then she called up the belief she wanted to change: the belief that her plane would crash. Initially, this belief was bright, vivid, and large in her mind. She deliberately changed the characteristics of the picture, making it dim, fuzzy, and flashing away in the distance. She replaced that picture with a new belief: that her plane would safely and successfully take off, fly, and land on the ground.

In her mind she saw the airplane soaring gracefully through the sky. She saw herself smiling, holding her husband's hand, and accepting peanuts from a gracious flight attendant. She actually felt the plane landing on the ground, bumping gently, and then gliding to a halt. She saw herself walking down the steps of the plane and collecting her luggage.

Suzanne was getting close to successfully changing her beliefs, but she wasn't quite there yet. The next step of the sub-modality change technique is to frame the new belief, not in terms of an end result but in terms of the process or the ability that will help you achieve and gain your goal. For Suzanne, this might mean seeing herself able to fly without anxiety and traveling to places around the world she has always dreamed about.

The last step of the sub-modality change technique is to do an emotional stability check to determine if there's any way your new belief could be a problem for you. Could it cause you any emotional conflict in the future? In Suzanne's case, flying more and traveling may take her away from loved ones she cherishes. Perhaps traveling more would not be something she would enjoy long-term, since it would take her away from people she loves spending time with. In other words, just because you are able to eliminate a fear of doing something doesn't mean you should automatically spend time doing it. I may be able to eliminate a fear of bungee jumping, but that doesn't mean I should engage in that activity on a regular or any kind of basis.

If you think ahead and know it would be good for you to have this new belief, then proceed. If you're not sure, use a concept called congruency that's incredibly effective in helping you decide whether a belief is emotionally good for you.

Congruency

Congruency basically says that you should evaluate a new belief from all three thought processes—seeing, hearing, and feeling—to determine if it will create any inner conflict or anxiety for you. For example, if your new belief is to be more assertive when people are taking advantage of you, you might see yourself responding in specific ways to people who do just that. When you plug into the three neurolinguistic thought processes, you'll *see* yourself being tough and demanding. That could mean the way you stand or walk or even the way you sit when you're in these situations. Auditorily, you'll *hear* yourself saying things in a very assertive way. Kinesthetically, you'll *feel* more confidence and greater strength in your communications with people. You'll be more assertive in letting others know how you feel.

On the other hand, if your boss is uncomfortable with this kind of confrontation, you might want to avoid acting on this belief with him. A compromise might be to weaken the current belief that you need to be assertive with everyone and instead to limit your assertiveness to people who don't have the power to hire and fire you. Or you might temper the picture of your assertiveness so that you don't respond to anyone in a way that would offend.

Let's try the whole thing from the beginning, starting with a belief that on some level you doubt you can achieve or sustain. Let's take, for example, the goal of pursuing a law degree. Your belief could be that the material will be too demanding or that you're too old. As you look at that belief, you should try to turn it into doubt by testing each mode of thought. Try to make it small, dim, and fuzzy. Any sounds connected with it should become soft, then inaudible, and you should also turn down the strength of your feelings about it, perhaps by using the disassociation technique we discussed in Chapter Three.

Use the sub-modality change technique to weaken the doubt you feel. Turn the image of you having difficulty learning into a flashing picture. When the flashing begins, immediately replace it with a picture of yourself successfully studying and concentrating on the information in front of you. See yourself smiling, reading a book, and gaining new, useful information. This would be a better representation than working long hard hours. Bring the positive image to the forefront and make it vivid, colorful, and detailed. As you do that, notice how the frame of the picture gets bigger and the image gets brighter and sharper. You might hear soft classical or jazz music in the background.

Notice the physiological changes you're experiencing. You should feel yourself smiling, feeling more joyous, more encouraged, and happier than ever about your goal. There will be other physiological changes occurring that you don't notice, but you should feel like a load has been lifted from your mind for one very good reason: Two strong conflicting beliefs about the same thing can't exist. You just have to weaken one belief before the other one can replace it. This technique simply short-circuits the process of eliminating non-supportive beliefs and doubts.

Now frame the new belief. To believe that you have the power to earn a law degree, see yourself as able to learn, having a great memory, and reading quickly. When the going gets tough, refer to this mental picture. It will reinforce the willpower you need to carry on as you'd originally planned.

Last, do an emotional stability check on your new belief. If need be, use the technique of congruency to evaluate your new belief from all three thought processes, seeing, hearing, and feeling. In gaining the confidence to pursue a law degree, you would imagine what the degree looks like, sounds like, and feels like, while at the same time making sure that being a lawyer is congruent with how you feel. I have a good friend who doesn't like being a lawyer. If he were to pursue more education for a new specialty, no matter how he was able to change his beliefs, it wouldn't change the fact that he doesn't enjoy practicing law. Congruency means that your beliefs have to correspond with what you love and enjoy already, as well as what you don't love and enjoy.

Replacing Non-Supportive Beliefs and Doubts with Supportive Beliefs

You can also try simply replacing non-supportive beliefs and doubts with supportive beliefs. You do this by moving from a belief to doubt, then contrasting the two, then testing the two, and then to the new belief.

Belief. Say you're good with people and believe that as a personnel manager you could effectively help your co-workers be more productive. You might represent this by seeing an image of yourself working side-by-side with one employee and then another, giving directions that will help develop win-win situations for both of you.

Doubt. Now, think of a doubt. Suppose your outcome is to become a department head in your company but, in spite of how good you are with people, you're afraid you don't have the discipline to lead thirty individuals. How would this be represented in your mind? It might be a picture of you acting confused and disorganized, not knowing what to do next.

Contrasting. Look at the differences between your pictures of belief and doubt. Notice the differences in brightness, vividness, color, fuzziness, how big each picture is, and whether it flashes.

Testing. Next, test each of these sub-modality differences, one at a time, to discover which is the most powerful in changing the doubt picture to belief. Perhaps going from a vivid to a dim picture has the greatest power over the doubt. Perhaps changing the color of the picture from bright primary tones to a dull grey does the trick and causes the doubt picture to flash or even fade away. Any one of the characteristics could do the trick; you just have to test each one.

New Belief. Finally, make sure you have a new belief in your mind with which to replace the doubt. If you doubt that you are disciplined enough to become a good manager, you need to replace that doubt with a new belief that gives you that power. See yourself learning ideas and concepts quickly. Make an image of yourself flying through books that seem complex to others. As you do this, remember to think of the new belief in positive terms only. Also, think of the belief as a process rather than as a goal or a delusion. A delusion would be having the belief that you can be wealthy and then seeing yourself as the richest person in the world.

The process of changing beliefs is very simple. Through the coming days, test your new beliefs to make sure the emotions and associations connected with them are consistent with the changes that have occurred. Do this by testing the visual representation of each of your beliefs. What does your belief look like after several days? Is it still vivid? Is it still big, colorful, and in the center of the picture frame? Does it still have all the characteristics that were there when you made it? You might have to reinforce it by going through these exercises again, but with practice you'll find the new belief integrated into your way of life.

Just remember that beliefs and goals need to be in harmony. If they are, you'll be able to work miracles the way the great violinist Itzhak Perlman did when one of the strings on his violin broke at the beginning of a concert. I've not been able to discover who wrote the short story that follows, but it is an incredible reminder of how powerful beliefs can be:

On November 18, 1995, Itzhak Perlman came on stage to give a concert at Avery Fisher Hall at Lincoln Center in New York City. If you've ever been to a Perlman concert, you know that getting on stage is no small achievement for him. He was stricken with polio as a child and so he has braces on both legs and walks with the aid of two crutches. To see him walk across the stage one step at a time is an awesome sight. He walks painfully, yet majestically, until he reaches his chair. Then he slowly sits down, puts his crutches on the floor, undoes the clasps on his legs, tucks one foot back, and extends the other foot forward. Then he bends down and picks up the violin, puts it under his chin, nods to the conductor, and proceeds to play.

The audience is used to this ritual. They sit quietly while he makes his way across the stage to his chair. They remain reverently silent while he undoes the clasps on his legs. They wait until he is ready to play.

But this time, something went wrong. Just as he finished the first few bars, one of the strings on his violin broke. You could hear it snap—it went off like gunfire across the room. There was no mistaking what that sound meant.

There was no mistaking what he had to do. People who were there that night thought to themselves, "We figured he would have to get up, put on the clasps again, pick up the crutches, and limp his way off stage, to either find another violin or else find another string for this one."

But he didn't. Instead, he waited a moment, closed his eyes, and then signaled the conductor to begin again. The orchestra began, and he played from where he had left off. And he played with such passion and such power and such purity as they had never heard before.

Of course, anyone knows it is impossible to play a symphonic work with just three strings. I know that and you know that, but that night, Itzhak Perlman refused to know that. You could see him modulating, changing, recomposing the piece in his head. At one point, it sounded like he was de-tuning the strings to get new sounds from them that they had never made before.

When he finished, there was an awesome silence in the room. And then people rose and cheered. There was an extraordinary outburst of applause from every corner of the auditorium. We were all on our feet, screaming and cheering, doing everything we could to show how much we appreciated what he had done.

He smiled, wiped the sweat from his brow, raised his bow to quiet us, and then said, not boastfully but in a quiet, pensive, reverent tone, "You know, sometimes it is the artist's task to find out how much music you can still make with what you have left."

Beliefs are powerful. Use the beliefs you have and change those that are self-sabotaging to achieve ever greater self-discipline in your life.

ASSIGNMENTS
Putting Self-Discipline to Work

1. Take one of the goals and outcomes you wrote down in Chapter Two and list both the positive and negative beliefs that either limit or empower you to achieve that goal and outcome.

    Then, replace each of the old non-supportive beliefs with new beliefs that will support your goals. Use the sub-modality change technique to do this.

2. Write down three of your beliefs that are based on future hopes and expectations and put a checkmark next to those beliefs that would support you in achieving a goal you have set for yourself. Then perform the belief check we've already outlined.

I played a tennis tournament recently at my club. One of my friends told me there is a definite home court advantage in tennis. I couldn't imagine that could be true, since there are no stadiums full of fans like there are in college football, save for the friends and relatives each of the players brings to the match. My friend mentioned that most people will lose while visiting another club because they believe it will be tougher to win and this creates a disadvantage. In this case, the belief doesn't support the goal. Ultimately, tennis players must believe they can win, or they have already lost.

If your goal is to get an MBA, a belief that would support that goal might be knowing that you're able to learn quickly and have a desire to gain knowledge. If your goal is to earn enough money to buy a house, your belief might be that you possess the ability to save money and don't need to live from paycheck to paycheck.

SECRET SIX

Achieving Self-Discipline by Using Contracts

> *I know a man who gave up smoking, drinking, sex, and rich food. He was healthy right up to the point when he killed himself.*
>
> Johnny Carson

Mark and Julie have a marriage that really works—for them. In this modern era of two-income families, where household chores are seldom divided among gender lines and men are as likely to cook dinner and do the dishes as women, while women are just as likely to pull out the toolbox and fix the child's wagon as men, Mark and Julie have settled on some old-fashioned behaviors that get the job done and satisfy them both.

They have three small children and Julie, by choice, is a stay-at-home mom. Since she's already at home and Mark typically doesn't arrive until shortly before six o'clock, Julie nearly always cooks dinner. She also cleans the kitchen up afterwards, while Mark plays with the kids and gets them in their pajamas.

Though Julie is imminently capable of heading out to the garage, sorting the recyclables, and loading them into the minivan each week, that's a job Mark usually performs. He also fills the birdfeeders, fixes and glues broken toys, and makes sure she has wood each morning to feed the woodstove during the winter months. He also sweeps up after bringing in each load of wood.

Julie does nearly all the cleaning. Mark will haul the heavy pail full of dirty diapers out to the laundry room for her if she asks, and he'll shake out the heavier rugs as well when needed, but she does all the vacuuming, dusting, and scrubbing of floors, walls, sinks, and toilets.

A carpenter friend of theirs, staying briefly with them during a home-improvement project he was helping with, commented to Julie one day that she "sure made things easy for Mark."

Julie was surprised. She responded, "He does a lot of things for me, too." The rewards of their system were tangible for Julie: Mark thoroughly appreciated her efforts in their home and Julie was relieved she didn't have to spend time working in the garage or fixing toys or tightening up the insulation in their drafty old farmhouse—areas she was less interested in and, in some cases, less proficient at.

The rewards for Mark were tangible, too: Though he was capable of cooking and cleaning, he was glad he didn't have to worry about doing it. His interests lay elsewhere, and he was able to devote his spare time to them and still come home to a clean, pleasant house and hot meals on the table every night.

Somehow, without ever really discussing it, they'd come up with an arrangement that worked for them both and they were both conscientious about holding up their end of the bargain.

Branch Rickey, former owner of the Brooklyn Dodgers baseball team, once said, "Luck is the residue of design." Designing this luck can begin with contracts. Though Julie and Mark in the story above might not have thought about it in these terms, they were using a subtle form of a contract to keep their home—and their satisfaction with one another—in top shape.

Contracts are nothing new to most of us. We're all operating under one sort of contract or another, written or verbal. It might be a contract to work each day for our employer. It might be an unspoken contract with our neighbors to keep our yards clean. It might be the understanding we have with our partners to be considerate and kind even when we're having a bad day.

Though most of us have an Achilles heel of one kind or another that makes it difficult for us to be self-disciplined, society's laws—another word for contracts—teach most of us to take responsibility for at least our social actions.

In this chapter, we'll focus on the use of a behavioral contract to help us develop the self-discipline we need to accomplish what we want in our personal lives. We'll also discover ways to reward ourselves for activities or behaviors we want to develop, behaviors that in turn will help us achieve outcomes and stay in control of our lives.

If you successfully complete the following four- to six-week behavioral contract, you'll find that commitment to your goals as well as your overall enjoyment and achievement in life will skyrocket. It shouldn't take longer than this, because by the end of four to six weeks your new behavior should be habitual.

This behavioral contract is really a promise or agreement you make to yourself to help you develop into the person you want to be, though ideally you'll involve another person as your self-discipline partner to help you increase your overall performance.

In turn, since it is well established that rewards are the most effective way to develop new habits or modify old ones, you'll reward yourself for keeping this promise or agreement. Ironically, most people use punishment as a motivation to change. While punishment can be effective to kill habits, it also causes resentment and ill feelings. Plain and simple, it's not as effective as rewards.

Rewards

The value of rewards shows up early in our lives, first in small things. For instance, as a child, your parents might have thanked you for making your bed or picking up your toys. They may have expressed pride in your grammar school achievements or showed up at your athletic events. Perhaps they set up regular play times for you provided your homework was done by a certain time.

Behavior Shaping

Your parents probably didn't think of it, but using rewards effectively is called behavior shaping. It works to mold and develop children and it can work to create self-discipline for you. There are four ways to shape your own behavior.

Four Ways to Shape Behavior

1. Apply a reward to a specific behavior
2. Withhold a reward linked to a certain behavior

Achieving Self-Discipline by Using Contracts

3. Apply punishment to a behavior
4. Consistently use the process of rewards to maintain a behavior

1. **Apply a reward.** Let's say you're trying to avoid eating between meals. It's hard to be a self-disciplined dieter because food itself is rewarding. You have a lot of trouble resisting, so you make a deal. If you stop snacking for a week, you'll reward yourself with a new dress or sports coat.
2. **Withhold the reward.** Withholding the reward can work along the same lines. For example, you know the bills have to be paid by the first of the month, but you are always late in paying them. Your utilities have even been shut off in the past because of your procrastination. It's not that you don't have the money; it's that you don't have the discipline to sit down and do your banking on time. So you make a deal with yourself that if you don't pay bills on a regular schedule throughout the month, you won't get to watch a TV show you really enjoy. (Of course, if you don't pay the bills and your electricity gets turned off, you won't be able to watch TV anyway.)
3. **Apply punishment.** Applying punishment is the third way to shape behavior, despite its obvious drawbacks. Suppose you need to study for a class an hour each night but you never get to it. You might punish yourself by doing an hour of yard work for every hour of belated studying. It's sort of a double whammy, but remember that this is not the most effective way to develop self-discipline. For one thing, if you don't have the discipline to study, you probably don't have the discipline to punish yourself for not doing it, either.
4. **Consistently use the process of rewards.** The fourth and most effective way to develop self-discipline is to consistently apply and withhold rewards in your life.

Performing a self-disciplined activity one time isn't enough to make it a habit. You must be consistent for several weeks to successfully shape a behavior.

With that said, the quicker you receive a reward, the greater the impact it will have on your behavior. Think about the games you play at carnivals or county fairs. You spend a dollar at a game and have a chance of walking away with a prize. How likely would you be to spend that dollar if you had to wait for your prize to be mailed? Not very.

We do work for deferred rewards, of course, such as waiting for an investment to pay off, but deferred rewards have the least impact on our behavior. This also means they have the least ability to create self-discipline. To be most effective, you need to use deferred rewards in conjunction with the behaviors you want to modify. Deferred rewards could come in the form of a bonus at the end of a year or a wall plaque recognizing your work or perhaps dinner out at the end of the week with your spouse, but only after you've reached certain goals for the week.

Behavioral Contracts

A behavioral contract that uses rewards will allow you to develop the self-discipline you need to achieve your goals. This means, first, that you need to determine which rewards hold the most pleasure and thus will be the most motivating for you. To do this, look at the worksheet below labeled "Rewards and Reinforcers." Listed on it are some of the things you might feel are treats or rewards for self-disciplined actions. Take a moment now and check which ones appeal to you the most. Also fill in the blank spaces on the bottom with any rewards you'd like to add to this list.

REWARDS AND REINFORCERS

Activities	IMPORTANCE	MEASUREMENT	FREQUENCY
Watching Television			
Listening to the Radio			
Cup of Coffee or Tea			
Being alone			
Reading a Newspaper			
Reading a Book			
Reading a Magazine			
Exercise (Jogging, Spa, aerobics)			
Hobby			
Long Baths or Bubble Baths			
Eating Favorite Foods			
Going to a Movie, Play, Concert			
Sports (Tennis, Skiing, Swimming)			
Going out for dinner			
Smoking			

Activity Checklist: Check the activities you do, whether you enjoy them or not.

Importance: On a scale from 1 to 10, how enjoyable, how important, how much do you like doing this activity (not necessarily in relation to the others checked)?

Measurement: When you engage in this activity, how much time do you usually spend? How much do you eat or drink? How many? (e.g., 2 hours, one-half hour, 1 cup or glass, 1 magazine, 1 apple, etc.)

Frequency: How often do you do this activity? (i.e., each day, twice per day, once a week, once a month, etc.)

Next, go to the column labeled "Importance." On a scale of one to ten, rate the importance of each reward to you with "one" being the least important and "ten" the most important. This rating is critical in effectively using rewards that work; only those activities you rate five or above are useful in creating self-discipline.

The next column is "Time Spent." This refers to the amount of time you spend doing an activity that you consider rewarding. Measuring the time you spend on an activity is important because it has a bearing on whether you'll use it as an immediate or deferred reward. Obviously, you wouldn't take a trip every weekend to reward yourself for doing something that week, but you might take a long walk as an immediate reward for completing an activity.

The last column is "Frequency." How often do you engage in an activity you consider to be rewarding? Again, this has a bearing on whether you'll consider it a deferred or an immediate reward and will help you decide which reward will be the most effective in reinforcing desired behavior.

Now look at the worksheet called "Behavioral Contracts."

At the top of this sheet are two columns labeled "If" and "Then." The "If" column represents the target behaviors you want to be more self-disciplined about. Fill in the "If" section with statements such as, "If I make six cold calls each day" or "If I book one appointment per day" or "If I read one chapter each day" or "If I stay on my diet each day" or whatever it is that you want to be more self-disciplined about.

When you've done this, go to the "Then" column. "Then" statements stand for the reward you'll get from changing your behavior and fulfilling the "If" statement. After an "If" statement such as "If I make five sales phone calls each day" you might write, "Then I can watch the evening news."

The "Then" part of the contract can but needn't be drawn from the Rewards and Reinforcers sheet. Any reward can be

Achieving Self-Discipline by Using Contracts

BEHAVIORAL CONTRACT

Effective Dates: From _____ To _____

If _____ Then _____
_____ _____
_____ _____

If _____ Then _____
_____ _____
_____ _____

If _____ Then _____
_____ _____
_____ _____

Bonus _____
_____
_____

Control: _____
_____
_____

_____
Signature of Goal Achiever

_____
Signature of Partner

This Contract will be reviewed on _____
Date

used if you've rated it at an enjoyment or importance level of at least six.

Directly beneath the "If" and "Then" columns is a section labeled "Bonus." The bonus is a reward for successfully accomplishing the weekly goals and activities you've set for yourself. This bonus could be something like giving yourself a dinner at a nice restaurant on Saturday night after completing a week's goals. Essentially, it's anything you think would be rewarding and would reinforce your goals in the future.

Directly below the "Bonus" section is the "Control" section. For this you'll need a partner. Choose somebody, ideally your spouse or someone you work with, who can help you enforce this contract and encourage you throughout the program. Since we humans often rationalize ourselves into a reward even when we haven't earned it, a partner isn't just a good idea but a necessary part of the plan to help keep you on track. Thus, this partner needs to be someone you see daily, someone who's truly supportive of you, someone who can discuss your goals and accomplishments with you, and someone who can commit to being supportive of your efforts for the next four to six weeks—essentially, someone who understands your goals and desires and wants them for you almost as much as you want them for yourself.

Don't set yourself up for disappointment by using a possible competitor as a self-discipline partner. There is a chance that if you select an office mate, they may see you as a competitor for a job they also want. If you suddenly improve your performance, for example, you may be that much closer to being selected for the position they also want.

When you approach your partner, you might suggest a two-way arrangement. If at some point your partner decides such a program might be a good idea for them, you'd agree to be their partner.

You need to interact with your partner about your progress on the program at least once a day. In addition, you need to complete a Weekly Activity Log that will enable your partner to see how much you've been doing. Set this log up by listing the days of the week, Sunday through Saturday, and next to each day recording the activity you engaged in that moved you closer to your goal.

You should also be prepared to do one more thing. To further help keep you committed to this program, write a check to your partner for two hundred dollars or more. If you fall short of your contractual obligations, if you fail to reward yourself when you've earned it, if you fail to interact with your partner, if you do not complete the weekly activities sheet, or if you decide to quit the program for any reason except because you've changed your goals, you forfeit the two hundred dollars to your partner. If you quit before the four- to six-week period is up, your partner must cash the check without your permission and spend it any way he or she sees fit.

Now select a goal you wish to start working toward during the next four to six weeks. If it's a major goal like making $100,000 a year, slice it down by dividing by twelve. This will tell you the amount you need to make each month, around $8,500. If you break it down further, you'll need to make about $2,000 a week. You could even break that down to a daily target if you like.

If you push yourself to do something, you'll always find an easier way to do it.

A computer accessory salesman with whom I worked had this goal: He wanted to own a Pearson thirty-one-foot yacht, which cost approximately $50,000. The salesman earned only about $2,000 a month. He made about two sales a week, eight sales a month, and his average commission was approximately $250. So you can see that it would be difficult, at best, for him to buy the yacht outright or even to lease it. He also set a goal for himself to purchase that yacht within two months. Since his goal depended on a larger income, he needed to increase his sales. His averages dictated that to get one sale he had to see about two prospects. To see two prospects, he had to book about three appointments. To book three appointments he needed to call on a referral basis ten people.

His average activity showed that he was calling approximately twenty people a week. He was booking about two appointments a day and seeing about two prospects a day, which yielded him two sales per week for a weekly grand total of $500. The lease on the yacht would cost him around $600 a month. For this salesperson, that meant generating about three more sales per month. This translated into calling thirty more referrals per month or about eight more referrals a week. He also would have to book nine more appointments and see six more prospects per month. This would have to be done over and beyond the number of sales he needed to maintain his current standard of living.

If this seems like a lot of work to you, keep in mind the law of forced efficiency. This holds that if you push yourself to do something, you'll always find an easier way to do it. In this particular example, the salesperson, when faced with making more calls, found easier ways to prospect including using referrals much more effectively. Eventually he wasn't doing that much more. He was just improving his efficiency, and as a result his productivity and income. He wasn't working harder; he was working smarter.

The way this individual started on his program was very simple. We knew how hard he was working in terms of activity—he was making around four referral calls per day, booking about two appointments per day, and seeing around two prospects a day. He was also making a sale on average every two days. Although he'd ultimately have to increase his activity, we started him at his current normal activity level to try to get him adjusted to the program.

His rewards and reinforcers sheet indicated that he enjoyed, on an importance level of six or more, watching television, playing tennis, and drinking coffee. He also enjoyed going out to dinner on the weekends. We decided to link the coffee drinking to phone calls. For every call he made, he could take a sip of his coffee. If he made no phone calls he received no coffee that day. Since he also liked to watch television in the evening, we linked television time (about an hour each evening) to appointments. If he went on an appointment he could watch television that evening. If there were no appointments that day, there was no television either.

If this seems harsh, don't believe it. It was all his idea. These were rewards he had been giving himself without earning them. On his new program, they became reinforcers that he used to become more self-disciplined.

The last reward linked to an activity was tennis. Since this individual greatly enjoyed playing tennis, but only a couple of times a week, we linked seeing prospects to playing tennis. For every two prospects he saw, he would receive an afternoon or evening of playing tennis. There was no reward given for the number of sales he made because if his activities increased, we knew sales would follow. The bonus for the salesman was that if he accomplished his goals for the week, he could go out to a nice restaurant as a reward.

During this individual's second week he increased his phone calls by one per day. It wasn't until the fourth week that he also increased his booked appointments as well as the number of prospects he saw during the day. By making a slow, steady increase, he was able to adjust to the extra activity while preventing stress and strain. He also adjusted to rewarding himself, or not giving himself rewards, depending on the activity he performed. He was slowly but surely developing self-discipline. By the sixth week he tripled the number of sales he was making because he tripled his sales activity. Later, it didn't take him long to maintain the higher level of sales even though he was working less. He just learned to work smarter and better. He bought his yacht for cash without even having to get a loan or a lease.

In another case, I worked with a manager who didn't seem to have the time to read more business-related articles and books. His target behavior was to develop self-discipline in spending more time reading, thereby increasing his efficiency in his job. His goal was to read one chapter per day, which he kept track of on his weekly activities sheet. He saw numerous benefits to his goal. By reading, he would get more information that would make him more valuable to his company. He would also be in a good position to directly increase his pay because of the new skills he would pick up through the reading. He would also develop more interest in his job because he would know more about the industry in general.

We started this manager off by putting him on a very simple program in which we encouraged him to read one more page per day. It usually took him only a minute or so to do this, but just getting the book out, looking at the page, and reading it was enough to start a habit of reading. In time we increased the number of pages he read. Most important at first was just getting a book in front of him.

We found from his rewards and reinforcers sheet that he enjoyed walking around the block at noon. On his importance scale, walking was an eight. So, every time he read one page at lunch, he could have his noon walk. After the third and fourth week, his goal was increased. He was rewarded with a walk only after reading five pages. His activity was slow and it took about six weeks before he was actually reading ten pages, or a chapter, per day. Once he met his reading goals on each of the five workdays, his bonus was playing eighteen holes of golf on the weekend.

Another salesperson I worked with at a major stock brokerage company hated prospecting. In fact, he flatly didn't do it and his business was at the point of failing. Even in the face of failure, he still wouldn't force himself to make referral or cold calls. I asked him what he liked to snack on in the morning. He told me bananas. So I linked the reward of one small piece of banana to every phone call he made. About a month later, after using the banana as a reward, he reported that his cold calls and referral calls had increased 150 percent! He thought it was silly, but every time he made a cold call, he'd give himself a small piece of banana. Even though it seemed childish, he still was able to associate a pleasurable experience, the fruit snack, with a non-pleasurable experience, the phone call. Getting on the phone became much more enjoyable.

> *If you push yourself too hard at the beginning, you'll burn out.*

Frequently, people using this method say to me, "Kerry, I'm smoking two packs of cigarettes a day, but my objective is to stop smoking and I want to stop smoking tomorrow. How can I use self-discipline to accomplish this?" The truth is, you need to have a systematic program by which you can change gradually and permanently. Without such a program, most people will never sustain the change.

Also, while I encourage you to increase your activity after your first week or so of using reinforcers or as soon as you feel comfortable with the program, you need to start your program at your present level of activity. Stay at that level for a week or two until you get used to the program and you've consciously committed to maintaining that level of activity. Then and only then should you move to increase your activity, and don't move on to the next level until you've grown accustomed to the current level. If you push yourself too hard at the beginning, you'll burn out.

For example, one salesperson who had been making no phone calls to get business began making one hundred calls per day. By the third day, he found he couldn't keep up the pace and he wasn't able to complete the program.

By the same token, I can't stress enough how important it is to take a reward when you've earned one and to take it immediately. Immediate rewards help you increase your activity much faster. Many individuals I have worked with give themselves a sip of fruit juice or maybe a couple of nuts for every phone call they make.

Another way to use an immediate reward to increase your activity or target behavior is by using tokens. After all, most of us probably shouldn't eat a piece of candy after every phone call. Tokens work equally well to give you an immediate reward at times when you don't want or shouldn't have your usual reward and can be such things as poker chips, pennies, or even paper clips.

For example, you can state on your behavioral contract that you will receive one token each time you say something nice to an employee or one token every time you ask for a sales referral. Each token might represent one half hour of television time or a cup of coffee. For every five tokens, you might receive time to play tennis or even an hour of golf. For every ten tokens, you might receive time reading just for pleasure in the evening.

Or, you might decide to use tokens as a means to help you develop self-discipline in getting to work earlier. At first you could give yourself a token just for leaving your house ten minutes earlier in the morning. Later on in the week or month, you'd give yourself a token only if you arrived on time. Still later you'd give yourself a token only if you were early.

A psychologist friend of mine used to work with the University of Michigan football team. The U of M Wolverines are among the best N.C.A.A. college football teams in history, but they weren't always so successful. Years ago my friend decided that tokens might be an effective tool to get Michigan's players to tackle harder, fumble less, and recover their fumbles more frequently.

The coaching staff, on the advice of the psychologist, started putting little stickers on the player's helmets for every big tackle they made or for every fumble they recovered. The ends and the wide receivers received stickers for every catch they made.

To their surprise, the coaching staff found that the players would do practically anything to get a sticker! They would jump over people, mow players down, practically go through brick walls to get one of those tokens. It's a lot like the Army giving stripes to denote rank or medals to award valor. It's basically a symbol of what each of us works for: recognition through a reward that all can see and admire. This is often more valued than money, which, by the way, is itself just another token.

By using a contract with yourself, one you've designed with rewards for self-disciplined behavior, you'll be surprised at how quickly your undesirable behaviors change. What's more, you can use this behavioral contract to change or reinforce any behavior you want. All you have to do is stick with it. When you do, you're keeping one of the most important agreements you'll ever make—an agreement with yourself to live up to your complete potential.

By using a contract with yourself, you'll be surprised at how quickly your undesirable behaviors change.

ASSIGNMENTS
Putting Self-Discipline to Work

1. The only assignment here is to page back through the chapter and fill out the worksheets. Start right now on achieving your dreams.

SECRET

seven

Achieving Self-Discipline by Using Meta Patterns

> *Whenever I watch TV and see those poor starving kids all over the world, I can't help but cry. I mean, I'd love to be skinny like that but not with all those flies and death and stuff.*
>
> Mariah Carey

One day the father in a very wealthy family took his son on a trip to the country with the firm purpose of showing him how poor some people are. They spent a couple of days and nights on the farm of what would be considered a very poor family.

On their return home, the father asked his son, "Well, what did you think of that family?"

"They were great, Dad," his son replied.

"Did you see how poor some people are?" the father asked.

"Oh, yes," said the son.

"So what did you learn from the trip?" asked the father.

The son answered, "I learned that we have one dog and they have four. We have a pool that reaches to the middle of our yard and they have a creek that has no end. We have imported lanterns in our garden and they have all the stars in heaven. We have a small piece of land to live on and they have fields that go beyond our sight. We have servants who take care of us, but they serve others. We buy our food, but they grow theirs. We have walls around our property to protect us, but they have friends to protect them."

With this the boy's father was speechless.

Then his son added, "Thanks, Dad, for showing me how poor we are."

ANONYMOUS

The father in the story above had a well-developed outlook on life. The life of a farm family was "poor." The life of a family living in the lushness of a city with all that money could buy was "rich." This man's meta patterns didn't allow him to realize that his perceptions weren't necessarily accurate—until his son stunned him with the perceptiveness of his comments.

What Are Meta Patterns?

Meta patterns are really an explanation of how we humans process information. Meta patterns are like an internal computer program that allows us to either generalize or store information, causing us to pay attention to or ignore certain bits of information that can affect our attitudes and perceptions. Meta patterns are the states of mind we automatically access as we work to achieve what we want out of life.

Achieving Self-Discipline by Using Meta Patterns

Once upon a time, an exasperated mother whose son was always getting into mischief finally asked him, "How do you expect to get into heaven?"

The boy thought it over and said, "Well, I'll just run in and out and in and out and keep slamming the door until St. Peter says, 'For heaven's sake, Jimmy, come in or stay out!'"

Jimmy, like most children, had well-developed meta and behavior patterns. The two can be closely linked. When my daughter Caroline was eight years old, she found that she couldn't compete with her older sister Catherine, then ten, intellectually or physically, but she did have other resources: She could cry and whine. When she wanted something or felt her sister was taking advantage, she would do a sort of cry/whine that was very effective in helping her get what she wanted. After all, Mom and Dad always came running.

> *Meta patterns are the states of mind we automatically access as we work to achieve what we want out of life.*

Catherine also found a behavior that worked in helping her get her way: aggression. When she wanted something, Catherine would just take it from her sister, which in turn caused Caroline to cry and whine.

Getting into mischief, crying/whining, and resorting to aggression are just three of the meta patterns kids commonly use. Adults use these meta patterns too, though less often than children. After all, adult meta patterns are more effective and very complex.

Meta patterns are more than just a taste for preferences in life, however. They're the drives that keep us moving in a certain direction, whether it's toward or away from something. Some of us move toward heavy physical exercise, for example, and spend time in gyms or outdoors jogging or walking. Others move away from strenuous physical activity. Still others move towards the arts by going to concerts, museums, or the ballet, while others shun everything except hoedowns in the barn.

Human beings display five types of meta patterns. Knowing what they are, how they influence us, and how to use them to our advantage is one highly effective way of achieving self-discipline.

Meta Pattern One: Moving Toward or Away

If somebody asked you what you wanted out of your career, your family, or your life, would you tell them what you wanted or what you didn't want? Likewise, does your cup tend to be "half full" or "half empty"? This tendency to move toward or away makes up the first type of meta pattern.

Someone with a "moving toward" meta pattern would answer the question in terms of what they wanted. Someone with a "moving away" meta pattern would answer the question in terms of what they didn't want.

To determine whether your meta state is one of moving toward or away, think about how you tend to answer the typical question most spouses and parents ask when you get home from work or school: "How was your day?" If your tendency is to answer "Great!" or some such variation, your meta state is one of moving toward. If your tendency is to answer somewhat negatively, such as "Not so good" or "Okay I guess" or "Rotten, as usual," your meta state is one of moving away.

I'm always amazed when I ask someone how they are and hear, "Things could be worse" or "So-so" and then hear others say, "Great!" or "Couldn't be better." Recognize the moving toward and moving away meta patterns?

You can also ask yourself how you decided to buy or rent your last home. Respond out loud if you can. If you answer that you decided on your current home because it had a beautiful view with a big yard or old graceful trees or something else positive about it, your meta state is one of moving toward an option. If you answer that it was the best of a bad lot or you liked it at first but wouldn't move there again because the living room is too small, your meta state is one of moving away.

Or, ask yourself how you decided to buy your last car. If you answer that it was the only one you could afford, your meta state is one of moving away. If you describe all the great things about it, your meta state is one of moving toward.

Recently I asked a friend what she desired from a date. She spent almost half an hour telling me what she didn't want in a man. She didn't want someone who was poor, who wasn't able to show her attention, who didn't spend a lot of time with her, and who wasn't tall, dark, and handsome. I understood what she didn't want, but I was still confused as to what she did want. I even asked her the same question again. It was interesting that she said, "I just told you, didn't I?"

Meta Pattern Two: Frame of Reference

The second meta pattern that makes up our attitude is our frame of reference. This frame of reference is either internal or external. For example, how do you know when you've done a good job on a project? If you know you've done well only when others tell you that you have, your frame of reference is external. If you have a gut feeling that your work is good no matter what anyone says, your frame of reference is internal. Pretty self-explanatory, isn't it?

I was thinking about beginning my MBA program a few years back when a friend said, "Are you nuts? You already have a Ph.D. You are really successful. You won't have as much time at home and won't be able to spend as much time with your kids. This is crazy; the time it will take you to study won't be worth it."

This reaction really threw me and for a time I didn't enter the program. If you have an external frame of reference, other people can knock you off your self-discipline program. If you have an internal frame of reference, you are more likely to stay focused on your goal.

To be more self-disciplined, we all need to have a greater internal frame of reference. To strengthen your internal frame, once you've set an outcome for yourself, measure every action you take against that outcome. This will help you resist external forces that might draw you away from it.

> *If you have an external frame of reference, other people can knock you off your self-discipline program.*

Another way to strengthen your internal frame of reference is to use the belief representations we talked about in Chapter Five. Try right now to re-access that picture of the belief that supports an outcome you have in mind.

For instance, if you're working on that MBA, imagine yourself breezing through graduate studies at the top of your class. Try to pay very close attention to the brightness, the size, and the vividness of the picture. Now go back to thinking about your outcome, getting the MBA. That outcome will occur if you stay internally focused. Then, every time you hear doubting comments, call to mind the picture of the belief that shows you have the ability to get that MBA.

Meta Pattern Three: Sorting

The third meta pattern involves how emotions are sorted. This basically concerns how we see ourselves in relation to others. If you sort only by yourself, you might be a self-absorbed, arrogant egotist. On the other hand, if you consistently sort by others, you might be an emotional martyr.

How does this meta pattern of sorting affect self-discipline? Again, as in the case of the external or internal frame of reference, if you sort by others exclusively, your meta pattern may sabotage your chances of becoming self-disciplined and staying focused on your objectives and outcomes.

For example, a man I knew who consistently shot himself in the foot in terms of his ability to achieve a high level of wealth did so because he was unable to control the degree to which he sorted by others.

Warren Harvey was brilliant and a hard worker. He was also a well-liked, generous man who could be counted on to quietly slip you a twenty-dollar bill from his pocket or to buy you lunch at the local café if you were on hard times.

His dream was to own his own real estate company and by the time he was forty years old, he had achieved this dream. Times were good, business was booming, and Harvey had soon employed a dozen or so support staff, as well as taken on a number of partners, individuals whose company he greatly enjoyed and who also desired great wealth.

Unfortunately, not all of the new employees or partners had Harvey's brilliance or work ethic, even though they were pleasant people to work with. When the economy took a nosedive and the real estate market fell off, Harvey worked harder than ever and continued to bring money into the company. But the money he brought in did just that: It went into the company to support all the various staff who were not earning their own keep. It did not go into Harvey's pocket, though Harvey spent money as though it did.

The years went by and the pattern continued. It wasn't long before Harvey had dug himself into a financial hole so deep that his wife had to go to work to help support the family. Twenty years later, she's still working to help extricate the family from debt, while Harvey's business goes on much the same as before, employing numerous staff who cost a lot and who bring in very little money, with Harvey working endless hours and bringing in just enough to keep them all going. Ironically, closing up shop and working for himself would bring him a level of wealth that would keep him quite comfortable, but he can't bring himself to do it. He feels responsible for all these people he's employed and doesn't want to let them down.

While the story of Warren Harvey might make it look like sorting by self is best, the best of both worlds is to be somewhere in the middle, leaning toward the sorting by self side. You can't and shouldn't ignore others, but it's important to keep focused on what you want and need.

> *The best of both worlds is to be somewhere in the middle, leaning toward the sorting by self side.*

Here are some questions to determine whether you sort by others or by self: What do you like best about your job? If you answer that it pays well or the hours are good or another self-centered reason, you are sorting by self. On the other hand, if meeting wonderful people is the reason you like your job, you probably sort by others.

Likewise, do you like to work with others or by yourself? If you answer by yourself, you probably sort by self. The opposite goes for you if you work best with others, but remember that sorting by others can harm your self-discipline. After all, if you have a deadline to get a project done but someone needs to talk to you, sorting by others could affect your ability to meet that deadline.

You can learn to sort by self by using the reward system we discussed in Chapter Six. For example, if you have a deadline and you're assertive enough to tell your friend that you'd love to talk after the project is over, you could give yourself a reward of golf on the weekend or a dinner for two.

Meta Pattern Four: Necessity or Possibility

The fourth meta pattern that affects our attitude is the tendency to be motivated by necessity or possibility. A heartwarming story about a little girl who is clearly motivated by possibility rather than necessity goes like this:

> Sarah, ten years old, wears a brace all the time because she was born with a muscle missing in her left foot. She came home one beautiful spring day to tell her father she had just competed in "field day" at school, where they have lots of races and other competitive events.
>
> Because of her leg support, her father's mind raced as he tried to think of encouragement for Sarah, things he could say to her about not letting this get her down. Before he could get a word out, she said, "Daddy, I won two of the races!"
>
> Her father couldn't believe it! And then Sarah said, "I had an advantage."
>
> Ah . . . The father knew it. He figured she must have been given a head start or some other kind of physical advantage.
>
> But again, before he could say anything, Sarah said, "Daddy, I didn't get a head start. My advantage was I had to try harder!"
>
> ANONYMOUS

A good way to discover how somebody is motivated is to ask why they bought their house. If they said they needed a five-bedroom house because they have four kids or because they needed a study to work in, they are probably motivated by necessity. Likewise, station wagon owners and van drivers are more likely motivated by necessity than possibility, while those driving VW convertibles or Porsches are more likely motivated by possibility than necessity.

> *Possibility people are motivated less by what they have to do than by what they want to do.*

Possibility people are motivated less by what they have to do than by what they want to do. They see a wide variety of choices, experiences, and options in life. They're very interested in knowing what they *can* have rather than what they *should* have.

In terms of your self-discipline outcomes, it's good to have a mixture of both of these tendencies. While your goals should take into account the necessities of staying committed, they should also include the possibility-thinking aspect of looking at new ways of how you can reach your outcomes more quickly.

Meta Pattern Five: Work Style

The fifth and last type of meta pattern involves your particular work style. There are three kinds of work-style meta patterns. The first is independent, the second is cooperative, and the third relates to proximity.

1. **Independent Meta Pattern**. The independent meta pattern is displayed in those who get a great deal of enjoyment from working on their own. These individuals like to work by themselves and take full credit for it. They're the sort who wish less to become part of a group than to run a group, and they may have difficulty working with other people.

   > *These individuals like to work by themselves and take full credit for it.*

   For example, if your meta pattern leans toward the independent side but you decide to campaign to be president of the local parent teacher association (PTA), you might be in trouble. Think of how bad this could be for you! As president, you are responsible to your constituency. You also have to lead and interact with those who hold positions in the PTA. You're independent and controlling, but you're going to have to work with others to get what you want done. Can you see the sparks flying already as you hear yourself telling them, "It's my way or the highway"?

You might be better off simply writing letters to the leadership of the PTA telling them how to better run their organization. At least then you wouldn't have to try to work with them.

2. **Cooperative Meta Pattern**. Individuals with a cooperative meta pattern want to be part of a decision-making body. They want to share responsibilities and activities. They're the sort of people who may not like to make a decision on their own so much as they like to get agreement from others before they commit themselves.

For example, if one of your goals is to read every evening but your meta pattern includes a cooperative, interpersonal mind set, you might find it difficult to spend that much time by yourself. The solution might be to read one hour each evening before joining friends.

Take another example: Every January I go skiing with about forty doctors from around the U.S. who form the Blue River Trauma Society (BRTS). We helicopter in to the rugged British Columbian/Canadian mountain range called the Cariboos. You have to be an advanced or expert skier to attempt this kind of risky adventure, but all the docs in the group have a wonderful time. One day, one of the docs wanted to go into the lodge because it was too cold. He complained a little and could have gone in anytime on his own, but instead he tried to get agreement from the four other people in the helicopter before he committed himself to stopping for the day. To see the cooperative meta pattern played out in front of my very eyes was both amusing and unmistakable.

3. **Proximity Meta Pattern.** The final category in this group consists of individuals who display a proximity meta pattern. This is a mixture of the first two types. These people like to work with others while maintaining control over a project. If this is your meta pattern, your attitude might be influenced by the kinds of projects you're working on.

A good example of the proximity meta pattern again comes from the BRTS group. The group's leader, an orthopedic surgeon named John Campbell from Bozeman, Montana, organizes the group every year for very little compensation. He is a member of the group but also the organizer. It is fun to watch him ride roughshod over what often looks like an ill-behaved fraternity yet still revels in the group's activities.

This proximity meta pattern seems to include the best of both worlds, for you get to enjoy others' company but you have the ability to run things or simply be by yourself.

Has this meta pattern business begun to sink in? Let's test it and see. Think about the last few U.S. presidents, beginning with President George W. Bush. Which meta patterns do you think he displays? Does he seem to move toward or away from issues? This is debatable, but he seemed to move away from many divisive issues in the beginning of his presidency until terrorism took front stage. Then he moved toward it, as the old saying goes, "like white on rice."

> *Individuals with a cooperative meta pattern want to be part of a decision-making body.*

Here's a tougher one: During Bill Clinton's scandals, do you think he sorted by himself or by others? He seemed to be watching the polls pretty carefully in the heat of his troubles, especially regarding the Monica Lewinsky issue. He also appeared to find amazing confidence after a poll showed the American people didn't want to see him impeached merely for an extramarital affair. Right or wrong, sorting by others seems to have enabled him to weather the calls for his resignation.

Last, do you think Ronald Reagan used an independent or proximity meta pattern? From presidential historians we have learned that he seemed to be great in front of crowds but didn't particularly like the day-to-day cabinet meetings. He was also famous for leaving much of the responsibility for various governmental workings to those he trusted. In spite of this, no one has claimed he wasn't a great leader. Rather, the argument has been made that sometimes leadership is manifested in motivating large groups rather than in interactions with only a few.

> *The good news is, we can attempt to change our meta patterns by distorting, deleting, or generalizing incoming information.*

It should be obvious by now that the meta patterns we display have a great bearing on whether we'll be successfully self-disciplined. Because of this, the self-discipline approaches we take either need to fit well into the meta patterns we already possess or we need to alter our meta patterns to accommodate the self-discipline approaches we are taking to achieve the goals we desire. The good news is, we can attempt to change our meta patterns by distorting, deleting, or generalizing incoming information. We all do this to some extent anyway as we deal with various situations. Why not consciously capitalize on it to help maintain self-discipline? As George Bernard Shaw once said, "If you can't get rid of the skeleton in your closet, you'd best teach it to dance."

For example, if your meta pattern is one in which you tend to sort by self yet a friend has a big office party coming up that she wants you to attend with her, you can distort the incoming information that causes you anxiety by telling yourself, "I will not be the only person at this party who doesn't enjoy big get-togethers. There will be someone else hanging out in the corner or the kitchen, and I will be able to escape there too when I need a break."

In another example, say you are an individual with a moving away meta pattern whose outcome is to get an MBA and you read an article that degrees of this type are no longer as important as they once were for getting a better job. Your automatic response might be to say, "Why am I killing myself working an eight-hour job and going to class at the same time?"

Instead, delete information in favor of your meta pattern and rationalize to yourself that there will always be great opportunities for qualified people, more so now than ever before.

Likewise, if you're having trouble staying on your diet, you could delete that particular bit of information and tell yourself that a little sacrifice now will be nothing compared to the joy you will have with a new body after a couple of months of dieting.

You can also generalize incoming information to help alter a particular meta pattern. For example, if your frame of reference is external and your wife has a business meeting out of town for the second weekend in a row, don't tell yourself, "This really stinks! I can't believe she's leaving again so soon! Now what am I going to do?"

Instead, say to yourself, "Despite how it appears right now, this doesn't happen very often and it means she's really doing well in the company. I'm proud of her and I know she will miss me, too, but this will be a good chance for me to get some much-needed work done around the house."

It can take some time to get into the habit of working with our existing meta patterns. Traumatic situations, though not desired, can cut through the chase and help us change our meta patterns quickly, as the following story suggests:

Some time ago a man punished his five-year-old daughter for wasting a roll of expensive gold wrapping paper. Money was tight and he became upset when the child pasted the gold paper on a box to put under the Christmas tree.

Nevertheless, the little girl brought the gift to her father the next morning and said, "This is for you, Daddy."

The father was embarrassed by his earlier reaction, but his anger flared again when he found the box was empty. He spoke to the child in a harsh manner. "Don't you know, young lady, that when you give someone a present there's supposed to be something inside the package?"

The little girl looked up at him with tears in her eyes and said, "Oh, Daddy, it's not empty. I blew kisses into it until it was full."

The father was crushed. He fell on his knees and put his arms around his little girl and begged her to forgive him for his unnecessary anger.

An accident took the life of the child only a short time later and it is said that the father was a changed man forever. He kept that gold box by his bed for all the remaining years of his life. Whenever he was discouraged or faced difficult problems, he would open the box and take out an imaginary kiss and remember the love of the child who had put it there.

ANONYMOUS

Using Meta Patterns Successfully

Regardless of which meta patterns you display, to use them successfully you need to keep in mind the following four tips:

1. **Recognize which meta patterns you possess.** For example, if you have a meta pattern that's typically moving toward things, then thinking about a great body is a better way to slim down than to think about losing weight. If your meta pattern is moving away, thinking about actually losing weight would be a more effective way for you to achieve your outcome.
2. **Use your frame of reference, whether internal or external, to support your goal and outcome.** For example, if your frame of reference is external, telling yourself you'd be a great candidate for a weight-loss program because of your concern about other's opinions would be a good idea.
3. **Change your belief systems to best utilize your existing meta patterns.** As you may find, meta patterns can be difficult to change. If your meta pattern is one of moving toward rather than moving away and your diet outcomes are focused on losing twenty-five pounds, there's a conflict. To make your meta patterns and outcomes congruent, you can use a belief in your ability to eat two small meals a day instead of three large meals. That's a way to modify the outcome to best use the existing meta pattern.
4. **Monitor yourself through your self-discipline change program.** Make sure you're actively focusing on information that supports your most effective meta pattern. For example, if your frame of reference tends to be external, make sure you don't let others discourage you. If your frame of reference is internal, you may want to insulate yourself from others and not tell them what your goals are.

I tend to move away from things rather than towards them. Another of my meta patterns is necessity rather than possibility. During the final stretch of my MBA studies, I found the course on managerial accounting so difficult I actually asked my CPA for help. John told me there are two types of people in the world: those who have a mind for numbers and those who don't. He advised me to drop out of the course until I had time to take another prerequisite, but I had invested too much time and trouble for that. Getting an A+ in the course didn't motivate me, but getting a D did. As soon as I was able to see how near I was to failing, I jumped into high gear, studying and cramming almost twelve hours a day until the final exam. I ended up with an A+ for the course, but it wasn't because I was trying to do well. I was trying not to fail.

Knowing my meta patterns enables me to concentrate on what is naturally appealing. For example, there are some goals in my life I want to just go out and grab. These include a better serve and forehand in tennis. There are also some problems I want to move away from. These include traffic tickets, flight delays, and behavior problems with my kids. Likewise, I love to speak to groups, but I hate airline flights. The carriers are increasingly passenger-unfriendly, the security is tighter, and it is becoming lunacy to be willing to spend ninety minutes waiting to get through a security line.

It would be easy to say that my career is too tough. (Recognize the moving away meta pattern?) Instead, I distort the airline experiences in favor of remembering the great places I travel to and the wonderful people I'm privileged to address. It helps to remember the following quote by Winston Churchill when I'm tempted to let situations and events beyond my control get to me: "A pessimist sees the difficulty in every opportunity; an optimist sees the opportunity in every difficulty."

In the final analysis, it's good to be aware of our meta patterns for one overriding reason: We can put them to work for us instead of against us, as the young executive in the following story eventually managed to do:

> A young and successful executive was traveling down a neighborhood street, as usual going a bit too fast in

his new Jaguar. He loved to drive fast, loved the rush of adrenaline it gave him. He was watching for kids darting out from between parked cars and slowed down when he thought he saw something.

As his car passed, no children appeared. Instead, a brick smashed into the Jag's side door. The man slammed on the brakes and drove the Jag back to the spot where the brick had been thrown.

The angry driver then jumped out of the car, grabbed the nearest kid, and pushed him up against a parked car, shouting, "What was that all about? What the heck are you doing? That's a new car and that brick you threw is going to cost a lot of money. Why did you do it?"

The young boy was apologetic. "Please mister . . . Please, I'm sorry. I didn't know what else to do. I threw the brick because no one would stop."

With tears dripping down his face, the youth pointed to a spot just around a parked car. "It's my brother," he said. "He rolled off the curb and fell out of his wheelchair and I can't lift him up."

Now sobbing, the boy asked the stunned executive, "Would you please help me get him back into his wheelchair? He's hurt and he's too heavy for me."

Moved beyond words, the driver tried to swallow the rapidly swelling lump in his throat. He hurriedly lifted the handicapped boy back into the wheelchair, then took out his fancy handkerchief and dabbed at the fresh scrapes and cuts. A quick look told him everything was going to be okay.

"Thank you and may God bless you," the grateful child told the stranger.

Too shook up for words, the man simply watched the little boy push his wheelchair-bound brother down the sidewalk toward their home.

It was a long, slow walk back to the Jaguar. The damage was very noticeable, but the driver never bothered to repair the dented side door. He knew he needed to keep the dent there so he'd never forget its message: Don't go through life so fast that someone has to throw a brick at you to get your attention.

ANONYMOUS

Ah, meta patterns. Thinking about what our meta patterns are and getting into the habit of putting them to our advantage to achieve greater self-discipline may take some effort, but it's effort that will more than pay off in the long run.

ASSIGNMENTS
Putting Self-Discipline to Work

1. Identify the five meta patterns you display and evaluate them to see how many support the goals and outcomes you identified in Chapter Two.
2. Think of your values and goals and try to come up with three new or modified outcomes that would fit nicely into the meta patterns you already possess.
3. Think about the possibility of altering your meta patterns to more successfully achieve your self-discipline goals. Is it possible to do that? What specifically would you need to do?

SECRET
eight

Achieving Self-Discipline by Coping with Stress

> *If you're going through hell, keep going.*
>
> Winston Churchill

In 1962, John F. Kennedy's assassination shocked the United States. A twenty-seven-year-old army captain led the funeral procession transporting his body as a mourning nation grieved the loss. One week later, that same twenty-seven-year-old captain died of a massive heart attack.

A seventy-five-year-old man bet two dollars on a long shot at the racetrack. When his horse won, he became ecstatic at the prospect of winning $1,600. He was so overwhelmed, in fact, that just as he arrived at the window to collect his winnings, he collapsed and died.

What do these two victims have in common? One was young; one was old. One died during a period of national grief, the other while feeling overwhelming joy. Yet they shared a common denominator: Both experienced significant stress just prior to their death.

Odd as it may seem, all change, negative *or* positive, causes stress. The more unexpected the change in habits or environment, the greater the likelihood that stress will affect us. Sometimes this stress is mental, sometimes it is physical, sometimes it is spiritual. Most significant of all, many medical researchers believe that seventy percent of all medical problems are stress related, yet only two percent of patients tell their physicians about the problems causing their stress.

Stress and Change

Stress not only accompanies every major life change we experience, from growing up to moving to a new community to aging, stress also accompanies the changes that occur as we embark on a self-discipline program and lose weight, increase our wealth, or alter bad habits. Ultimately, this stress often diminishes our commitment, causing us to lose the motivation necessary to continue our self-discipline regimen. The irony of self-discipline is that the more successful we are at implementing discipline in our lives, the more change we will experience.

A life insurance agent friend of mine doubled his income in 1984. It shot up so fast, in fact, that he employed ten new administrative people to support him. He was able to spend more time with his family and experienced great pride in his achievement. Yet in November of that year, he contracted mononucleosis. Bedridden for three months, his business was soon near bankruptcy. Nearly a year later his wife left him, taking their three-year-old son with her. Stress was as much a factor in his setbacks as was his illness. His life had changed too quickly for both himself and his spouse.

In the short term, many causes of stress seem obvious. A prospect you are close to selling won't return your phone calls. A customer won't return the necessary paperwork after you have spent many months working with him. Perhaps you have office employees who move so slowly they seem more like monolithic structures than alert human beings.

Our response to stress is fairly predictable, as are the four stages of behavior we go through during stressful situations: alarm, resistance, adaptation, and fatigue. Say a client of many years is approached by a competitor and ultimately becomes convinced that the product you've sold him is obsolete and a bad investment. When you discover the transgression, you experience shock and alarm. How could this happen? How could your customer be so stupid as to listen to other people?

The next stage you experience is resistance. You may contemplate bombing your competitor's building, or at least slicing his tires. You may walk up and down the hallways of your office complaining to everyone you see. You may feel yourself tensing more and more as you talk about your situation. After writing letters to well-chosen recipients, you decide the best thing to do is to call the client and explain to him how he was wronged.

Then you begin to adapt. You rationalize that it might be more work to pursue your former client than it is worth. You may even contemplate ways of preventing the problem in the future.

The final stage you experience is fatigue. Even though you learned of the replacement only a few hours ago, your whole body feels like a twenty-ton truck ran over it. Every muscle aches, and you're mentally exhausted and emotionally spent.

The consistent theme in this example is that the more time you spend resisting the stressful situation, the more fatigued you will be in the end. Likewise, the more strenuously you resist, the more fatigued you will be. If you've ever arm wrestled, you know that each competitor tries to pin the other's hand and arm onto the table and that each experiences one common result: exhaustion after the match.

In the late 1970s in Linz, Austria, I competed in a tennis tournament against an Austrian hometown champion. "Boris" was favored to win the tournament. In fact, the tournament directors tried to ensure his championship win by entering him in the semi-finals without his having competed in the preliminary rounds like the rest of us. It was common, in those days, for a celebrity to receive money "under the table" to entice him to show up. This appearance stipend was often more than the winner's purse. Boris won the first set. I was ahead five to three in the second set when Boris tossed the ball up to serve. But instead of serving the ball to me, he served his racquet. He threw his tennis racquet across the net and it went whizzing over my head.

> *The more time you spend resisting the stressful situation, the more fatigued you will be in the end.*

My alarm stage set in. I felt shocked that this would actually happen. I then resisted. I ran over to the chair umpire and demanded that Boris be ejected from the match, but the tournament directors weren't about to expel an investment property as valuable as their champion. I then adapted by realizing my efforts at retribution were useless. I walked back onto the tennis court and stood ready to play, but I felt exhausted, as though I had already played a five-set match. I had spent so much energy resisting the situation that I had fatigued myself. I was unable to play effectively throughout the rest of the match, and Boris went on to win the second set seven to five and take the match.

Types of Stress

There are two distinctive types of stress. Canon stress is named for the esteemed physiologist Walter Canon, and Selye stress is named after the great Canadian endocrinologist Hans Selye. Both types of stress work on the presumption of a weak link. Every one of us has a weak link physically or mentally. This weakness is the first part to break, and because of this no two people will react to stress alike. Some may have heart attacks while others, like me, lie awake with insomnia night after night.

Canon Stress

Canon stress, also known as the "fight or flight" response to stress, is based on the notion of a physiological reaction to stress. This type of response is useful during periods of emotional or physical threat. If you are a caveman and are attacked by a saber-toothed tiger, for example, Canon stress will help you climb a tree quicker than a cat.

During periods of physical threat Canon stress saves lives, but except for these unusual examples it also serves to take lives. Physical symptoms of Canon stress are as follows:

1. **Muscle pain or illness**. Have you ever come home at the end of a bad day at the office feeling as if you've been run over by a Sherman tank? You may have been suffering from Canon stress. Even if you didn't lift more than a pencil, the constant tensing and relaxing of muscles can leave you feeling as if you have run a marathon.
2. **Tension headaches**. Unlike migraines, this type of headache is caused by the tensing of skull muscles. Often aspirin can help relieve this pain, although relaxation techniques are more effective in the long run.
3. **Irritable stomach**. Because the stomach muscles are also in tension, digestion continues in the form of acid

release. The acidic content causes ulcerations in the stomach lining.
4. **High blood pressure**. Because of the automatic tightening of muscles, even the capillaries are affected. Blood pressure is increased by blood being redirected away from the extremities toward the torso, putting pressure on the heart.

Some of the psychological symptoms of Canon stress include:

1. **Intractable fatigue**. This is a condition in which one is actually too tired to sleep. After I have traveled through time zones, I sometimes find my exhaustion is so great that I am literally unable to fall asleep.
2. **Insomnia**. Because the muscles in the body are kept in such a state of tension, the body can't relax enough to fall asleep. Insomniacs often report being caught in a "Catch 22" cycle of stress. They become so afraid of not sleeping at night that their anxiety levels soar, causing even more severe insomnia. You may experience this during periods of pressure at work or at home.
3. **High irritability levels**. Bobby Knight, ex-basketball coach for the Indiana Hoosiers, once threw a chair onto the court during a game because of his high irritability level due to tension. His temper got him into more trouble later when he was accused of choking a player for being disrespectful to the coach. He was fired for violating a zero tolerance policy the athletic director had initiated to curb violent outbursts.
4. **Lack of concentration**. If you have ever flown, you have undoubtedly sat for long periods of time in an airport. Did you try to read or concentrate? During this high-stress time of waiting for a flight, it becomes difficult to concentrate or follow through on a thought. You

are instead paying attention to flight announcements and watching your belongings.
5. **Acute anxiety**. The psychological discomfort caused by stress stirs up apprehension and anxiety, occasionally to the point of fear.

Selye Stress

The second type of stress, Selye stress, works in a different way. Also reacting to perceived change, this type of stress serves to effect problems with other systems in the body.

Some Selye stress symptoms commonly experienced include:

1. **Migraine headaches**. These headaches cause more pain than simple headaches; it often feels as though pain is wrapped around the head or centered unilaterally in one area. Such headaches can result in flu-like symptoms. Once they begin, it becomes difficult to break the cycle of pain that sets in.
2. **Rash or skin eruptions**. You have undoubtedly seen people red-faced when upset. Others actually break out into a facial rash during stress. I worked with one person whose face turned red when stressed. I usually knew how much stress she was under just by looking at her blotchy skin.
3. **High vulnerability to illness**. Selye stress lowers the body's natural resistance to illness. If you have had the flu or a cold more than once this past year, you may be suffering from stress.
4. **Heart disease**. This is often due to coronary artery obstructions, causing damage to the heart itself. The arteries are somewhat elastic vessels. They need to be elastic to allow blood to ebb and flow. Selye stress literally causes these flexible arteries to harden, making

them susceptible to stricture and blockages. Arteriosclerosis is a hardening of the arteries made worse by stress. It is interesting to note that a majority of heart attacks occur between 8:00 and 9:00 A.M. on Monday mornings. Apparently, job stress is a great contributor to heart attack episodes.
5. **Cancer**. I never understood the true magnitude of how cancer can be affected by stress until I watched what happened to my mother. In 1979, even though she had never smoked a single cigarette in her life, she had a lung removed because of cancer. In February of 1987 she collapsed in her home, paralyzed with a malignant brain tumor. Thankfully, her neurosurgeon was able to remove all of the cancerous tissue. After the operation he said that the cancer, latent for twelve years, had been activated because of stress. One theory is that cancer develops because the body's resistance level is fatigued by stress, making us more susceptible to cancer attacks. Another theory is that the normal resistance to cancer we all have is diminished by constant stress.
6. **Gray hair**. Even if you've been using Grecian Formula for years, you may be surprised to learn that the pigment of hair called melanin is destroyed during stress, leaving hair a premature gray.
7. **Male pattern baldness**. Baldness is obviously hereditary, but it also can be accelerated during periods of high stress. The smooth scalp muscles may actually constrict the hair follicles, causing the hair shaft to fall out more quickly.

The psychological symptoms of Selye stress include:

1. **Depression**. Defined psychologically as loss to oneself, depression can trigger periods of hopelessness and helplessness. Serious depression can lead to suicidal thoughts. Over seventy percent of the adult population

in America reports serious depression at least once a year. Interestingly, the highest number of suicides in our society occur between the ages of seventeen and twenty-five years, the ages in which there is radical physical and emotional change.
2. **Psychosis**. Many psychologists believe that all of us possess latent psychotic tendencies. The line between normality and abnormality is a thin one. Stress-related pressures can push us across that line, causing ordinarily normal people to exhibit very unpredictable and unstable behavior.

Stress and Behavior: Type A and Type B

Your personality type also contributes greatly to your stress level. Consider this question: Does your behavior help you or hinder you in your efforts to achieve your goals? Do you roll with the punches or make things worse for yourself? Take the short test below to determine your personality type. If you answer "Yes" to ten or more of these questions, consider yourself a Type A personality. If you answer "Yes" to fewer than ten of these questions, breathe a sigh of relief and consider yourself a Type B personality.

TEST FOR STRESS

1. Do you finish others' sentences before they do?
2. Do you move, walk, or eat quickly?
3. Do you prefer a summary instead of skimming or scanning a complete article?
4. Do you become upset in slow lines of traffic?
5. Do you generally feel impatient?
6. Do you find yourself disinterested or unaware of details?

7. Do you try to do two or more things at once?
8. Do you feel guilty if you relax or take a vacation?
9. Do you link your worth to quantitative tangibles like income, company growth, or number of employees?
10. Do you try to schedule more and more activities into less and less time?
11. Do you think about other things while talking to someone?
12. Do you exhibit nervous gestures like drumming your fingers or tapping your pen?
13. Do you continue to take on more and more responsibility?
14. Do you accentuate key words in ordinary speech when there is no reason to do so?
15. Do you work hurriedly even though deadlines are not pressing?

Type A Personalities

A textbook example of a Type A person is Barry, a successful, hard-working salesman. Barry likes his work very much. Indeed, Barry is so proud of his sales achievements that he keeps constant reminders of his current production on his desk. He is continually trying to increase his sales volume by working harder and harder and he spends increasing hours in the office. As if that weren't enough, he uses a stopwatch to track production and often yells to his secretary, "We have three minutes left to complete this project." He also finds that his secretaries don't last long on the job. But when one leaves, Barry says, "I didn't really like her anyway."

Barry has trouble coping with traffic jams. He can't muster enough patience to wait in lines, even in fast food restaurants. He rarely has time to attend family gatherings. He tries to motivate newcomers in his company by appealing to their great desire to achieve and he makes every effort to set a good example by never complaining to his colleagues, but in private he will unload his gripes to his wife about how a customer or business associate has upset him. He admits feeling stressed, especially about things he cannot change.

Recently he visited a doctor who told him that his blood pressure and cholesterol count were too high. The doctor recommended that he watch his diet and learn to relax. It was easy for Barry to decrease his cholesterol level by cutting down on butter and eggs and other dairy products, but try to relax? Fat chance. To do nothing, or be engaged in what he considers "non-productive leisure," would be too uncomfortable to him. Barry has begun jogging to keep his heart going, but he's unaware that his arteries are clogged from the long-term effects of cholesterol and the chronic bombardment of hormonal secretions released by his constant anxiety.

> *Twenty percent of stressed patients contracted eighty percent of all cases of heart disease.*

Barry's chances of leading a normal life and reaching a ripe old age are practically nil because Type A people like Barry run a higher risk of heart attack than Type B people do. In fact, Type A's are twice as likely to contract heart disease in addition to the higher levels of both anxiety and depression they feel.

Cardiologist Meyer Friedman in his book *Type A Behavior and Your Heart* discovered in 1981 that twenty percent of stressed patients contracted eighty percent of all cases of heart disease. He also determined that these individuals had a seventy percent greater chance of contracting heart disease than other patients. In short, these people had a greater tendency to feel stress and possess psychological and physical pain from that stress and were much more likely to decrease their life expectancy simply because of their personality characteristics.

Type B Personalities

Type B individuals, of course, react much differently than Type A's to life's challenges. These individuals are more relaxed but still highly productive people who have profitable, long-lasting careers. Type B individuals examine their own behavior often to determine when and how they can change. They are sensitive to the needs of people around them. They are also more open and friendly and often more cooperative than Type A's. They are not as time conscious, yet they seem to be aware of the correct time. In short, they handle stress well and yet manage to get a lot done. Unfortunately, they often seem to be in short supply.

Coping with Stress

Now onto the good part: how to deal with stress. It is practically impossible to totally eradicate stress, but we can learn to cope so well that we cause our performance to improve rather than deteriorate, even under the most stressful conditions.

Subjective Unit of Discomfort Scale

Managing stress begins with knowing how much stress we have. Look at the Subjective Unit of Discomfort Scale, or S.U.D.S. on the following page, to help you measure your physical and psychological response to stressful situations in increments from 0 to 100. Each of these subjective units (0, 5, 10, 15, 20, 30, and so on) also corresponds to symptoms you may have as a result of stressful situations.

 A low-stress situation, such as having a relaxing drink as you are about to fall asleep in front of the fireplace, measures 0. High stress situations measure 100, such as following

Achieving Self-Discipline by Coping with Stress

S.U.D.S.
SUBJECTIVE UNIT OF DISCOMFORT SCALE

MOTIVATION RANGE

Psychological Fear Range

- 100
-       You experience total panic.
- 90
- 80 You feel increased anxiety.
- 70 You feel an increase in problems like insomnia, free-floating anxiety, and depression.
- 60 You feel psychologically induced or psychosomatic illnesses such as ulcers and diseases.

(limitations to productivity)

- 55 You feel severe psychological discomfort and pain as well as headaches and muscle aches.
- 50 You feel psychological pain and experience emotions like irritability, bad temper, and a lack of concentration.
- 45 You feel anxiety and exhibit avoidance behaviors such as procrastination, tardiness, and a lack of motivation due to fears.

Maximum Performance Range

- 40
- 30 *This is your peak performance range.* Time flows quickly, enjoyment is at a peak, and you're very creative, innovative, think quickly, and make good decisions.
- 20 Motivation sets in. You're interested in seeing people and engaging in some productive activities.

Low Motivation Range

- 15 You feel low motivation for activities such as driving to work, reading a book, or taking a walk.
- 10 You're awake but totally comfortable, very relaxed, and contemplating going to bed.
- 5 You're drifting off, about to fall asleep.
- 0 Total relaxation—you're asleep and experience a complete absence of anxiety.

a group of Hell's Angels on the freeway with your car horn stuck.

What levels of stress on the S.U.D.S. scale do you experience during an average day? What are your lowest and highest levels? If your S.U.D.S. level is generally higher than 45, it's too high and you may suffer symptoms of burnout. If your S.U.D.S. level drops below 30, it's too low and you may experience "rust out." The following chart will give you a good idea of the symptoms you may experience. If you can keep yourself between 30 and 45, you will stay in a "peak performance" range. Everything will flow, you'll lose track of time, and you'll do your best work.

When I play tennis, my S.U.D.S. level is always between 30 and 45 and two hours feel like five minutes. When I'm prospecting for new business, I enter this range when I start to enjoy the telephone calls. But if I let my discomfort rise above 45, I will perform more poorly in selling situations. The same is true if I decrease my discomfort below 30.

Progressive Relaxation

One extremely effective technique for decreasing your S.U.D.S. level to a manageable level is called progressive relaxation. Nearly everybody who successfully copes with stress applies some form of relaxation technique to decrease their body's response to stress. Many salespeople pay enormous amounts of money to be hooked up to a biofeedback machine in order to help them relax. The technique I'm about to explain serves equally well in relieving symptoms and producing more relaxation.

The first step in this simple procedure is to make sure you are comfortably seated. Then, tense and relax your muscles as you inhale and exhale, mentally moving through every general area of your body, starting with your ankles and feet and slowly moving all the way up to the muscles in your head. As you pause in each general area, tense for a period of three seconds while you inhale and exhale, then relax the muscles and release.

After you've completed this step, imagine yourself at the top of a staircase with ten steps. Feel yourself inhaling and exhaling slowly with each step as you start from step one and descend all the way down to step ten, becoming more relaxed with every step. When you get to the bottom of the staircase, imagine yourself beneath an oak tree in a grassy meadow. Hear the birds chirping in the tree and the wind blowing softly through the leaves. Leave yourself under the tree for five or ten minutes. Imagine yourself so relaxed that you actually fall asleep for a short time. When you are really relaxed, you will experience a slight feeling of floating and muscle relaxation.

To come out of this state, see yourself at the bottom of the staircase again, this time going up three steps. With every step, take a breath in and let a breath out. With every breath, you will become more aware of the things around you. After the third step, open your eyes. You should be very alert, very aware, and very comfortable.

If you do this every day for the next six or seven days, you will be able to bring your body down to a fully relaxed, stress-free state. Many people who have used this technique are able after two weeks to simply picture the meadow and tree and feel more relaxed. This technique can be especially useful in meetings or when you come face to face with a co-worker or customer who gives you a tough time.

P.Q.R.S. Technique

A second technique for dealing with the effects of stress is called the P.Q.R.S. technique, which stands for prepare, question, relax, and solve.

Prepare. Without question, being prepared for a potentially stressful situation helps you to cope with it. If you know you have a meeting tomorrow morning with a difficult prospect, get eight hours of sleep and eat a good breakfast beforehand to help keep your stress at a manageable level. Also make sure you take a Vitamin B complex of B1, B3, B6, and B12 and decrease your intake of coffee, tea, or other stimulants.

Question. We know that if we resist stress or stressful situations we will feel more fatigued afterward. In other words, the effects of stress will be much more debilitating.

So, question your response. Is the situation really worth getting upset over? Is it something you want to make an issue of, knowing full well that the stress you receive from fighting it might not be worth the hassle or the resulting benefit?

Relax. Plan to spend five minutes out of every ninety simply sitting in your office, walking yourself down the staircase and into the meadow, and lying under that tree. If you do this, you'll find that your productivity will increase because you will think more clearly and concisely.

Solve. It's not the elephants that get us; it's the mosquitoes. The little things that eat at us bit by bit, every day, eventually cause our anxiety balloon to burst. But if we engage in a problem-solving campaign to make sure the little things don't defeat us, we will be able to manage them with ease.

Progressive Massage

A third technique for dealing with stress is called progressive massage. The best place to apply progressive massage is at the base of the neck and the tops of the shoulders and where the spine meets the head. When you eliminate stress here, you eliminate stress in your mind. You might ask your spouse or a friend to give you a massage, or you might even give yourself a shoulder and neck rub. I recently saw a chiropractor for back pain who specialized in deep muscle massage. He mentioned that he often sees fairly sedentary office workers with tight knots in their back and arms, all from the effects of stress. Kneading these knots out is a painful process depending on how much of the muscle is tied up.

Resource Circle

A fourth technique for dealing with stress involves using a resource circle. Simply concentrate on a time or an event in which you were completely successful. The event could be winning a sporting contest or giving a brilliant speech or receiving an award. In your mind, draw an imaginary circle on the floor or ground next to you. Now try to access that past event. Try to see it. Try to hear the sounds around you as if you were there and try to invoke the feelings you experienced when the event originally happened.

When you believe you are as close as possible to reliving the event, take a step into that imaginary circle. Then step out and repeat the exercise, recalling the event as it sounded, looked, and felt. Now do it again without recalling the three senses. Just step right into the circle. You should be able to immediately access that winning experience just by stepping into the circle.

I recently spoke to a man who told me he felt horrible about being overweight, but his patience and self-discipline had come to an end. He looked at his S.U.D.S. level and realized it was at 65. He remembered the resource circle technique and mentally drew his circle on the ground and stepped into it. Not only did his S.U.D.S. level go down to a peak performing level, he was able to reach inside himself and pull out strength he did not know he had. He reached his weight loss goal by controlling his anxiety.

Like this man, the most powerful coaches, business people, athletes, professionals, and scientists are those who, on cue and largely unconsciously, put themselves into a powerful state by giving themselves certain signals. Many are able to do this in spite of horrible things that occur in their lives, whether it's ill health, financial breakdown, family problems, or other tragedies. They can keep themselves in a successful resource state by triggering powerful mechanisms in their minds.

Attachment

One additional technique you can use to control anxiety was introduced in Chapter Three and is called attachment. Many athletes with performance anxiety use this to compete at their best. For example, before beginning a race, a competitor will put her hands on her hips to access past relaxation or a past success before kneeling down to the starting blocks. A 400-meter dash is an enormously stressful endeavor. Many racers lose before they start with a huge expenditure of anxiety in the minutes leading up to the race. But when an athlete can put her hands on her hips and calm herself down, she can gain control and put herself in a position to win.

Coping with Worry—Another Form of Stress

What if that customer decides not to buy? What if you can't lose twenty pounds in time for the annual dinner? What if next month's sales are as bad as this month's? What if you fail to make the bonus you earned last year? What if? What if? What if?

Stress and worry go hand in hand. If you can control the latter, the former decreases as well.

A wise philosopher once said, "Worry is the interest paid on trouble that is not yet due." In spite of this, we humans spend a lot of time worrying. Some psychologists believe worry is a natural neurosis that indicates a lack of security bred by childhood feelings of inadequacies. Other psychotherapists such as Alan Loy McInnes in his book *Power Optimism* believe that we are victims of the media who make money by whipping up feelings of worry in all of us.

One thing is certain: Worry paralyzes all of us, perhaps most especially the best and the brightest. If you are serious about implementing self-discipline in your life, you are a likely candidate for worrying. After all, worry is an indication that you are motivated, concerned, and serious about making changes in your life for the better.

Authors Mary McClure Goulding and Robert L. Goulding in their book *Not To Worry* believe that worrying is a waste of time but they also believe that worriers are "helped along" in their destructive behavior by three types of people: rebels, reassurers, and caretakers.

Rebels are a worrier's worst nightmare. They are the types who try to give the worrier something to really agonize about. They stay out late, refuse to call in, purposely make mistakes in financial records, drive recklessly, or refuse to get medical attention when the worrier deems it necessary. When Mom says to make sure to eat a good breakfast every morning while at college, the rebel instead drinks it by downing a can of beer. When a man tells his wife that her driving scares him, she drives extra fast.

Reassurers try to perpetually cheer up the worrier. They say things like, "Everything will work out, so don't worry." Or, "Your worries have never been proven out. You always figure something out." Reassurers seem like the reincarnation of Mom. In fact, many worriers call her often to hear this kind of empty but welcome encouragement. Some reassurers even try to dispel the worry with well-thought-out facts. They say things like, "You've worried about this same issue for the last three months and nothing has happened yet." But even this sort of factual discussion has little effect on the chronic worrier.

Caretakers spend much of their time taking care of the anxieties of the worrier. They install extra locks on every door. They make phone calls confirming appointments or heading off potential fears. They try to gain control for a worrier of situations in a world that can never be controlled.

The first step in coping with your worries is to figure out where you fit into this scheme. Are you primarily a worrier, a rebel, a reassurer, or a caretaker? Then, modify your behavior accordingly. If you're a reassurer, avoid asking the worrier to discuss her worries. You wouldn't ask a hypochondriac to talk about his medical maladies, so why do it with a worrier? Try to point your conversation away from areas the worrier is liable to "take off on." Another great technique is to direct the conversation away from worry and instead into success. Most of us try to change the subject when our children harangue us to buy something or to let them go out against our wishes, and the same technique works with worriers.

> *When we are able to be thankful for our problems as well as our successes, worry ceases to hold much credibility.*

The second step in coping with worries is to have faith. Since the idea of faith is explored in Chapter Eleven, I'll leave it alone for now. Suffice it to say that when we are able to be thankful for our problems as well as our successes, worry ceases to hold much credibility.

Is it realistic to completely exist without worry? Only if you don't care. All of us worry from time to time, but often worry depends on how much control we allow events and experiences to have over us. Those with a high degree of self-confidence tend not to worry as much as those who have a lower level of confidence. Highly self-confident people tend to think of their circumstances as manageable.

They believe they can work with a situation and make it successful. Those without such a high degree of self-confidence tend to think of circumstances as in control of them. They are less likely to believe they can make lemonade out of lemons.

Alan Loy McGinnes outlines five characteristics of people without worry that all of us can strive to emulate:

FIVE CHARACTERISTICS OF NON-WORRIERS

1. **They aren't often surprised by trouble**. They are realists who understand that trouble is what builds us and that how we deal with it results in the growth of personality.
2. **They have control over their future**. They have the confidence that things happen because they choose to let them happen.
3. **They allow for regular renewal**. Their growth is important to them to such an extent that if they don't grow, they die emotionally.
4. **They are cheerful even when they can't be happy**. You have probably heard of the phrase, "Fake it till you make it." This was obviously created for the optimists among us. They don't wear paste-on smiles but instead realize a bad situation can be improved if they are enthusiastic while they're in it.
5. **They accept what can't be changed**. Optimistic people constantly learn new ways to deal with their problems. They also are confident that their goals needn't change, just their methods of achieving them. Worriers and pessimists are often so stubborn in their plans that they resist and rebel. They then complain about how unfair things are when their intransigence causes them to fail.

    Worry is contagious but not incurable. Worry is learned, not inherited. Granted, if you have spent a lifetime learning how to worry it's difficult to learn to be optimistic, but if worry is interest paid before it's due, now's the time to close the bank account.

Coping with the Stress of Not Having Enough Time

Unfortunately, there's something more that causes us stress: a lack of time. It seems that no one has enough of it anymore. The man in the short tale below is typical of men and women both:

> John, a successful salesman in his early forties, is trying to apply the self-discipline techniques he has learned. He is now riding the exercise bike for thirty minutes every morning. He watches his caloric input and decreases his carbohydrates. But in his work life, things are rough. Today alone, John needs to process the paperwork on five more sales by noon and has another ten issues to iron out with his home office. He is falling behind in his customer calls and can't even get the standard paperwork done. His wife is losing patience with him, claiming he isn't the man she married, and he hasn't spent more than ten minutes with his kids in the last week. All this, and he can't even claim he's making more money.
>
> John feels more and more stressed as the week goes on. It doesn't make sense. He is becoming more disciplined and getting more done. He is more effective at work than even a month ago. He should be able to coast a little. But his work is more demanding than ever and he's enjoying it less.
>
> He rationalizes that he will eventually make more money, as if money will make up for the stress, but even that isn't happening yet.

If you are like the majority of professionals, your company probably isn't considering hiring staff to support you. In fact, they are likely thinking of whom they can fire to increase return. Can they get another two percent output and increase their revenue?

There are only two ways to respond: Learn to cope with stress by using the techniques in this book or by taking a course, and get smarter about getting things done. We all have the same amount of time; we just choose to prioritize it differently. Luckily, we can use the following six techniques to deal with the pressure of not having enough time.

SIX TECHNIQUES FOR DEALING WITH THE TIME CRUNCH

1. **Stop fighting self-created fires**. If you are spending more than twenty-five percent of your day fixing problems, you may be causing them in the first place. A few years ago, a client told me his business was hurting because he didn't have sufficient time to spend gaining new customers. I analyzed his day hour by hour and determined that he indeed wasn't spending enough time marketing. He was instead fixing computers, fighting overdue notices, and generally rectifying mistakes by his own staff. Surprised, I worked backwards and learned that he hired good people but only gave them minimal training and then sent the new hires to the wolves. Training after the first day was conducted only after a mistake was made. The problem was, the same wolves kept coming back to bite him.

Poor training creates poor motivation and poor motivation creates black holes of wasted money. The lesson is simple: When you hire someone new, take at least twenty-five percent more time to train him or her than you think is needed.

You can use this concept regardless of whether you're in business or not. After all, many of the fires we fight are a result of waiting until the last minute to do what needs to be done. Use the self-discipline techniques we have learned so far to start tasks earlier. For example, my wife adjusts all the clocks in our house ahead by fifteen minutes to make sure she is on time. In a way this is ridiculous—we all know the clocks are fast. But the results speak for themselves. We all pay attention to the fact that the clock is ticking and we'd better be ready.

Also, try to fight fires only in the afternoons. This may not work for critical emergencies, but in general you can train your staff to bring issues to you only during certain windows of the day. The alternative is to fight fires all day long and lose productivity as a result.

2. **Remember that if you aren't working daily toward *your* goals, you are helping someone else achieve theirs**. Keep your short (in the near future), medium (in the next three to five years), and long-term (more than five years away) goals on your desk in plain view. It is easy to fall into the trap of maintaining your business or your life instead of growing it, but maintenance of the status quo today will mean deconstruction tomorrow. Make time to build your business and your goals every day.

> *Make time to build your business and your goals every day.*

After all, if you are trying to work on your golf swing, do you only practice it the day you play a golf round? If you are trying to spend more time exercising, do you let two weeks go by since your last walk? Do you sell only when you are desperate and procrastinate making calls when business is good?

While it is often difficult to begin less appealing activities, try giving the most undesirable jobs the highest priority. Helen Gurley Brown, founder of Cosmopolitan magazine, said she always did the most unpleasant things on her list first to get them out of the way.

If all this sounds trite and obvious, you've been jaded. The winners in any industry who are regularly in the top five percent stick to their daily goals like glue. They review them in the morning before the day starts and plan out the next day before the current one is done, always with their goal in mind. They also hold planning sessions monthly, trying constantly to stay on track. This doesn't mean they never derail, but when they do take a detour, it's only a short distance back to the main track.

Do you sell only when you are desperate and procrastinate making calls when business is good?

3. **Sharpen your axe**.

Ponder this instructive tale:

> A lumberjack stayed home one day rather than go out with the other lumberjacks to cut wood. They ridiculed him for his absence and told him that he'd simply fall behind if he didn't come. The next day he cut twice as much wood as all the others. When the other woodcutters saw this, they asked what had made him so much more effective. The lumberjack simply answered, "Yesterday I stayed home to sharpen my axe."
>
> ANONYMOUS

I spoke at a large convention a few years ago in the mortgage business. Sally Ride, the first female astronaut in space, was the keynote speaker. My presentation was in the afternoon and I arrived an hour early that morning to get a good seat in the auditorium of 1,500 plus seats. 150 people showed up out of the 3,000 registered for the conference. What did Ms. Ride have to do to attract an audience? Catch a bullet in her teeth?

Compare that to the Life Insurance Industry's Million Dollar Round Table (MDRT) annual meeting. I spoke at their

June 1998 meeting of six thousand. There were exactly six thousand seats in the auditorium. If you weren't there by 8:00 A.M. you didn't get in. No one was late. No one was in the foyer chatting or in their hotel enjoying a late breakfast. People came to get an edge, to get better. To sharpen their axes. By the way, just to be *invited* to the MDRT your income for the preceding year had to be at least $150,000. Obviously, most in attendance made far more.

4. **Remember that a messy desk is a sign of a messy mind**. You should never waste time looking for items that should be at your fingertips. Keep essential items neatly organized. Only handle messages once. Read each e-mail and immediately answer it, file it, forward it, or discard it. Do the same with your mail. That way you won't have to read it twice.

5. **Stop sitting at your sit-downs**. Have you ever noticed how much time is wasted in meetings you didn't want to attend in the first place? Start holding them standing up. Meetings stay focused and end quickly when people don't relax so much that they digress to other topics.

Another good idea is to schedule appointments and meetings at odd times. If you schedule a meeting for 10:00 A.M., most people will expect it to last until 11:00 A.M. unless otherwise stated. If the appointment is at 10:20 or 10:17, you will appear to be busy and professional and the meeting will automatically carry the expectation of being short.

6. **Don't get trapped into the "Hurry Sickness."** Do you rush around even when you don't have to? Do you become impatient in lines even on Sundays? Do your thoughts turn to work on your time off? If so, you are suffering from "Hurry Sickness." Dr. James Dobson had a spot on his *Focus on the Family* radio show a short time ago in which a prominent psychologist described this malady. He talked

about a focus so intense that even time off becomes "time on." Be aware of whether this tendency lurks inside you. If it does, deliberately choose to behave differently.

It's abundantly obvious that stress can rob us of the pleasure we could otherwise feel, but it doesn't have to. Instead, we can increase our self-discipline to get more enjoyment out of life by using the techniques in this chapter to control stress, control worry, and cope with the time crunch we all face. When we do, we'll not only be happier individuals, we'll also be healthier ones.

ASSIGNMENTS
Putting Self-Discipline to Work

1. Try to measure your stress on a daily or even hourly basis by putting yourself on the S.U.D.S. scale at regular intervals. As needed, use the techniques mentioned above to decrease your stress. One great way to do this is to put a drop of fingernail polish on your watch. Whenever you look at the time, the polish will remind you to check your SUDS level. If it's too high, you can use the techniques above to decrease your stress and discomfort.
2. Identify three situations that are causing you stress. You may be thinking that you don't feel all that stressed. It's sort of like the old saw about the frog: If you put a frog in boiling water, it will quickly jump out. But if you put the frog in cold water and slowly heat it up, it will boil to death. You are that frog. You need to prevent stress from having an adverse effect on you today. Begin by applying the various techniques of Progressive Relaxation, the PQRS Technique, Progressive Massage, a Resource Circle, and Attachment. Feel free to overlap on the techniques as you attack your stresses.

SECRET
nine

Using Self-Discipline to Build Wealth

> *Every morning I get up and look at the* Forbes *list of the Richest People in America. If I'm not there, I go to work.*
>
> Robert Orben

Back in 1932, Charles Darrow was jobless and broke. His wife was expecting a baby any time. Though he was a heating engineer, there were no jobs available in the pit of the great depression. Darrow was just barely eeking out a subsistence on odd jobs from those who would hire him as a handyman. Times were bleak, but the Darrows had courage and tenacity. They laughed at their poverty, literally.

In the evenings, as an escape from their troubles, they made up a little game as a diversion from their depressing existence. Pretending they were millionaires and recalling pleasant vacations in nearby Atlantic City, they reconstructed the area adjoining the Boardwalk. Darrow carved hotels and houses out of small pieces of wood. They called the game Monopoly, and the rest is history.

Self-discipline can pay off in many areas, and one such place is in wealth building. This is a goal nearly everyone needs to be interested in, because according to U.S. government statistics, only fifteen percent of baby boomers have saved enough money to retire when they turn sixty-five. What's more, actuaries currently report that if you are under fifty now, you will likely live to be ninety. That means you will be in the retirement bracket nearly as long as you are in your income earning years. Most baby boomers have done little goal planning, choosing instead to put the hard choices off.

It gets worse. Not only do Americans have the smallest level of personal savings in the industrialized world, they also spend more than they make. The level of consumption has even outpaced the growth in income. The poet E. E. Cummings might have been speaking for many of us when he said, "I'm living so far beyond my income that we may almost be said to be living apart." Without financial goals, you may well live out your retirement years on a subsistence level social security income.

On the other hand, research at Yale University years ago showed that the three percent of students who set goals for their careers achieved more financial success than the remaining ninety-seven percent of the class who failed to plan.

Just look at the following statistics collected in *Are You Normal about Money?* by Bernice Kanner:

For ten thousand dollars, fifty-nine percent of Americans would allow their heads to be shaved.

For a million dollars, sixty-five percent of Americans would live on a deserted island for a year, sixty percent would take the rap for someone and serve six months in jail, and ten percent would lend their spouse for the night (sixteen percent more would consider it).

For ten million dollars, twenty-five percent of Americans would abandon all their friends and leave their church. An equal number would enter prostitution for a week. Last but not least, seven percent would commit murder. Seven percent. *That's one out of every fourteen people.*

Kanner makes the point that many of us would do just about anything to get money. Yet less than half of us, forty-nine percent, pay our credit cards in full each month to avoid interest. Only forty-three percent of Americans say they stick to a monthly budget, and only an equal number even have a budget set up. Only eighteen percent of workers contributed to a retirement account in the year 2001, and of the 401K participants, only fourteen percent put in the maximum allowed.

Kanner also notes that thirty percent of husbands and wives don't know how much their spouse makes. Even more shocking is the number of Americans who would rather become rich than find the love of their lives: according to Kanner, a full ninety-two percent of us. What this says about our society is something I'm not prepared to explore here.

The real shame is that all it takes to become rich is to follow a few simple rules: Acquire no credit card debt. Invest ten percent of your income every year. Max out your retirement accounts every year. Live within your means.

Of course, living within our means is easier said than done. We Americans have created a consumptive society that weans us to the tune of "Acquire, acquire, acquire." And acquire we do, everything from designer tennis shoes to the finest CD collection in town to four-wheel drive sports utility vehicles to high cholesterol from eating out too much.

Few of us can actually pay cash for everything we buy, so we put the rest on credit cards. Some of us even rationalize using such cards by telling ourselves, "Well, it's my new card and it has such a low interest rate that I just couldn't afford to pass the _____ (new dishes, Calvin Klein jeans, baby clothes, skateboard. . .) up." The logic here is absurd, but most of us have used it, or are using it even now.

Often, when our credit limit is maxed out or when we realize how deep is the water we're swimming in, we try to play the game of shifting our various balances to newer cards with lower rates. The problem is, those rates are usually only good for a brief introductory period and then we're slammed once again with high rates that, month after month, add hundreds or even thousand of dollars onto our existing debt.

A friend recently told me that he and his wife have agreed not to use their credit cards any longer unless they have the cash to pay the balance in full at the end of the month. Of course, they have to pay off their existing debt before they can implement their new plan, but it's a good one nonetheless. They've also decided to put one hundred dollars every month into an investment plan—something they've not done before, beyond the basic investment plan my friend has at work.

When I asked what had compelled them to make this decision, my friend told me his wife's parents, a retired couple in their early seventies in good health, are so deep in credit card debt they've had to sell their home—the home their children were raised in and the home they'd assumed they'd live out their retirement in.

The predicament his in-laws are in has so frightened him that he talked to his wife about changing their ways while there's still time to extricate themselves from the debt they've already created for themselves.

My friend said, "You know, it's not like we really need all the stuff we buy anyway. How many CDs can you listen to? How many sweaters does someone need? Do kids really need twenty different video games to play and every Barbie doll on the market? Can't we visit the library instead of buying every new book that looks good? Besides, I'm less and less confident we're going to be able to retire and live comfortably. We need to save more—and that means spending less."

Sounds good—as long as my friend sticks to his credit card plan, invests consistently, and doesn't try to play the stock market. As ludicrous as it sounds, Kanner reports that more than half of those investing believe they can beat the stock market averages, even though sixty-six percent of investors can't name a single stock in their mutual fund.

It's a little like the student who told his professor he would do anything to pass the class. Wash the teacher's car, his windows, rake his lawn, even baby-sit. But study? Forget it!

The bottom line is that if people were more diligent about their finances, they wouldn't have to resort to bizarre behaviors to get money. It all boils down to self-discipline. Many Americans spend enormous amounts of money on the lottery and other forms of gambling to gain quick riches, but the real wealth is in their own backyards. All most of us need is the willpower to make wise choices about money and to stand by those decisions.

> *The key to creating and accumulating wealth is the ability to establish a game plan to build wealth and then to follow that regimen.*

In short, the real magic isn't in finding a quick investment scheme, but in laying down a financial plan and sticking to it. Virtually every time I speak to experts such as financial planners, insurance agents, financial advisors, and bankers, they mention that the key to creating and accumulating wealth is the ability to establish a game plan to build wealth and then to follow that regimen. They also tell me that when people have problems with their money, it's usually because they disregard the advice of the professionals they pay to tell them what to do with that money.

Ed Williams, a financial planner in San Diego, California, is one of the experts I interviewed. Ed told me the story about a client of his named Phil. An electrical contractor,

Phil made a gross salary of nearly $800,000 a year. His net worth was about six million. He paid a $3,000 fee for Ed Williams' consultation and the resulting financial plan. He mentioned to Ed during his financial planning session that he was very concerned about paying taxes on his accumulated investments.

Phil did not implement Ed's suggestions and instead put $200,000 into a pharmaceutical company, thinking he'd take advantage of research and development loopholes in the tax laws to gain tax benefits. He also put $100,000 into a movie industry limited partnership. Both of these were extremely risky investments, yet promised very lucrative returns of thirty percent to fifty percent within just a few months.

The result of these investments was disastrous. The pharmaceutical company went out of business and Phil never got a penny back. The movie industry limited partnership didn't make one solid cent over five years.

Phil could have made a great amount of money if he'd put his funds into the vehicles Ed Williams had suggested. For example, if he'd invested his money in a fairly conservative variable annuity investment, Ed calculated he'd have doubled it within five years. Unfortunately, Phil wasn't disciplined. He wanted quick money and greed won over prudence.

When Ed heard about Phil's problems, he asked him to come in again so they could reestablish the financial plan but Phil seemed intent on turning his errors into disasters. He bought real estate instead and got burned in the sinking market of the early 1980s. He was like a Las Vegas gambler who doubles his next bet after a loss. Ultimately, his real estate investments foreclosed because he didn't have the money to carry them through a bad market period.

Moral number one of this story is that self-discipline is as important in making money as in keeping it. Moral number two is that, when it comes to making money, it's more important to hit singles than home runs. Wade Boggs was a batting master. When he needed a base hit he got one. This didn't mean he couldn't hit home runs, but a team doesn't win when nine players try to hit home runs. Likewise, people committed to self-discipline slowly and steadily increase their wealth instead of investing willy nilly in whatever get-rich-quick scheme comes along.

Financial planner Dennis Renter of Newport Beach, California, told me that more than two-thirds of the people making highly-leveraged investments lose money. It often seems that the people who are trying to accumulate wealth speculate while the people who are most concerned with protecting wealth build it.

Thus, it should come as no surprise that those who build up their investments are those who are most disciplined about it. Those who want money right now are the least disciplined because they're looking for a quick fix. Dennis says an investor's biggest temptation is big money promises from fast talking salespeople. He consequently trains his clients to answer people selling investment tools with, "I don't make any decisions on my own. Will you show this to my financial advisor?"

> *When it comes to making money, it's more important to hit singles than home runs.*

The following four-step approach is my advice to you in developing financial self-discipline and putting yourself on the road to slow and steady wealth.

Four-Step Approach to Financial Self-Discipline

1. Get advice to reach your desired outcome.
2. Plan to reach that outcome.
3. Develop a belief in your plan.
4. Review and reward yourself for staying on that plan.

   1. **Get advice.** The financial market has many intricacies. You'd do well, no matter what your background, to consult

with someone who's got a background in investing and the ability to be objective about what to do with your money. You can locate a financial planner by looking through the International Association of Financial Planners Directory, also called the Registry of Financial Planners, but that's just the beginning.

You need to feel confident with your advisor's experience and comfortable with her style. To get to this point, cooperate in all the interviews the expert conducts and be as honest as you can about your financial position and objectives.

This is a good time for you to share your outcomes with your planner, telling her what you want from your investments in the next five, ten, and twenty years. You also need to let her know how you see yourself reaching those outcomes.

Remember that outcomes aren't simply goals. They're the representation of how you'll feel and what you'll see and hear when your goals are realized. By sharing outcomes with your planner, you'll stay more committed to your financial plan. That's because your commitment is to a lifestyle instead of simply to money. Many investors lose money because they lose sight of the outcome they want to gain through investing. They simply concentrate on the money and greed becomes the single most important motivating factor for their investment strategies.

Make sure that you share your professional values with your financial planner as well. Tell her what you plan to do with your money after you're gone, whether it's to leave it to family or to charitable causes. Let her know what's important to you and how you plan to address those concerns.

There are three ways you can pay for this financial advice. The first is through commissions the advisor is paid based on the money you earn from the products she sells you, but this approach is risky since it carries with it a great motivation to sell you products rather than a plan that is right for you.

A safer approach is to pay for financial advice through asset management. Here, the advisor is paid one to two percent of your assets under management. In this scenario you have the confidence that whatever the investments your advisor recommends, she stands to gain little unless they pay off. The negative to this method is that your portfolio starts out every year with a minus two percent return due to the fees the advisor will take.

The third way to pay for a financial advisor is to buy a financial plan. Usually these tailored plans run from $2,500 to $5,000 for an initial set up.

Before you decide what to do, ask yourself how many times you have bought advice that you didn't implement. What is important is movement and implementation, not just knowledge. Unless you are already enormously self-disciplined, it is preferable to ask someone to supervise your investment activity. Remember, people usually don't fail by making the wrong investments. They fail by making *no* investments.

2. **Plan.** The financial planner will be of great help in helping you slice down your outcomes into steps you'll be able to take, but this person's help is only as good as the information he gets from you. Tell him how much risk you think you can handle and be realistic. There's pleasure and pain involved in investing. While the greater the risk the more you stand to gain, there's greater volatility, higher stress, and more uncertainty in high-risk investments as well.

> *People usually don't fail by making the wrong investments. They fail by making* no *investments.*

As you plan your risks, make sure you mentally picture yourself as committed and self-disciplined in working toward your outcomes. If you can see yourself carrying out your financial plan in a disciplined and orderly way, you'll be able to withstand the temptation to make quick changes based on the emotion of the moment. This isn't to say you should remain inflexible about which vehicles to use to achieve your outcomes, but I do recommend that you use enough self-discipline to consult your financial advisor before you make any changes. That is what self-discipline is all about—sticking to your plans until they need to be modified and then doing it with an eye to the future as well as the present. If your outcomes are consistent, you'll be able to maintain a plan, even if it includes changes in strategy.

3. **Develop a belief.** One of the major reasons people lose money is that they sabotage their own financial plans. It's obvious that Phil, the unsuccessful contractor, didn't fully believe in the power of his plan. That's why he acted to dismantle it in favor of something he did believe in. Though it takes discipline to stick with a plan and you will have occasional moments of doubt, if you believe in your plan you should be able to stay with it.

To help yourself figure out where you stand, do a belief image check to make sure your belief system supports your financial plan. Specifically, try to get a picture in your mind of what it will be like to have the power to stay with this particular financial plan for a couple of years. See yourself carrying out the actions you've agreed to. Be aware of any images of doubt that might be present. Is the belief in your plan big, vivid, colorful, and centered in your mental screen? If it isn't, manipulate the image to make it that way, or change the part of your plan that seems small, black and white, and fuzzy.

If you're not comfortable with the aggressive investment program you've discussed with your planner, you may well see a less than brilliant picture. Modify the program and see how that goes along with your outcomes as well as your belief. Since your mind represents self-discipline in terms of an image, you need to make sure that your desired outcome is big, vivid, colorful, and as centered as you can make it.

If you think you might simply lack what it takes to maintain self-discipline in achieving your objectives, you can address that as well. Evaluate this image of doubt and how it's represented in your mind. Is it an image of a weak beggar in the streets, or just a picture of a run-down house in a bad neighborhood? Whatever it is, look at its visual characteristics. Weaken each of them until they flash away. Don't forget to replace them with a strong image of your ability to maintain self-discipline. You might even slip in a picture of you keeping a budget or resisting a quick-money scheme. This belief-modification exercise will help you keep your commitment because of its power to help you focus on what's valuable.

4. **Review and reward yourself.** Don't forget to use the techniques of review and reward. This is the really fun part of your financial plan. Virtually any investment advisor will tell you to keep track of your investments and to maintain your plan to make those investments grow. This is foundational advice, and while it doesn't mean keeping track of the hourly stock updates, it does mean looking at your whole portfolio on at least a quarterly basis. This will help you determine whether your investments need to be re-evaluated to help you achieve your outcomes by the desired date.

These reviews need to end in rewards. Remember earlier when I mentioned that you don't fail by making the wrong investments; you only fail making no investments? The idea of "dollar-cost averaging" dictates that if you invest regularly and consistently, your return will be maximized. This means that if you invest when the market is down, you will be able to buy more shares. If you invest when the market is up, you will be able to buy fewer shares but they will be worth more.

How do you know when the market is up or down? You don't. That is why you have to invest consistently. Since 1929, if you missed just three stock market increases, you also missed seventy percent of the market return more consistent investors gained. You simply can't predict or time the market. Only consistent investing builds wealth. Thus, you should reward yourself every time you invest. Go out to the movies. Get a massage. You should think of investing not as taking a risk but as investing in your future. This act of consistent investing is what you should celebrate. The reward could also be something you outline at the beginning of your investment program to help keep yourself going every time you reach a certain point.

Ed Williams has a five-step self-discipline game plan to help virtually anybody accumulate enormous amounts of wealth, but it works only if people are willing to commit themselves. This five-step formula is based on common sense but is fueled by self-discipline.

Five-Step Wealth-Building Formula

1. Establish a goal for your investment program.
2. Determine which of your current assets you'll use to begin your investment.
3. Adopt dollar-cost averaging.
4. Review progress from investments every three months.
5. Diversify assets.

1. **Establish a goal for your investment program.** Whether your goal is providing an education for your children or retiring with a million dollars in savings, the trick is to decide how much money it will take to reach your goal and when you want to reach it. Visualize yourself in the future and ask yourself how much income you want when you retire. For example, if your goal is to retire ten years from now on a pension of $5,000 per month, you would simply work backwards, calculating what your investments will need to produce every month to meet your goal by that

date. You'll probably need help from your financial planner in doing this, but either way, remember to calculate the return on your investment ten years in the future as well as to adjust for inflation.

2. **Determine which of your current assets you'll use to begin your investment.** How much money do you have right now in stocks and bonds? Do you have mutual funds? What are your real estate holdings? Do you have a valuable collection of fine art? If you own your own business, what is it worth?

3. **Adopt dollar-cost averaging.** This is simply a very disciplined approach to putting money into an investment no matter what happens. The stock market will either go up or down—it rarely stays the same. With dollar-cost averaging, if you're disciplined, you'll make money no matter what the market does. For example, if the stock market goes down in value and you've made a commitment to invest $1,000 a month, you'll simply be able to buy more shares. When the market goes up in value you'll likely buy fewer shares, but those shares will be worth more.

Boom times in the stock market never last forever, but neither do the busts. Most of the financial planners I've interviewed say that during a ten-year period, the stock market will have three good years, three bad years, and four average years. With dollar-cost averaging, you'll make money on your investments no matter what the market does if you're disciplined in committing a specific amount every month.

A woman who's now a millionaire housewife made a commitment ten years ago of putting $500 into a mutual fund every month. She was effective because she was so disciplined. Speculators, on the other hand, sometimes seem to be throwing mud at a wall to see what sticks. Their effectiveness doesn't begin to compare to this woman's approach. She invested on a much smaller scale but it worked because the issue is not picking stocks. The issue in creating and accumulating wealth is having the discipline to steadily and consistently invest.

Sales great John Savage was a living legend in the insurance business. Deceased in the early 1990s, he was a member of the Million Dollar Round Table for forty years as well as a member of the Top of the Table, the best of the top insurance agents in the world. John said the death of a woman in his hometown of Toledo, Ohio, was the subject of discussion for weeks. The woman was found dead in her house and as police searched, they found more than $600,000 in trash cans on her property. An accountant John was meeting with a few days later ridiculed the woman, commenting on what a stupid place she chose to keep her money. "It's almost as bad as keeping money under a mattress," he said.

> *Boom times in the stock market never last forever, but neither do the busts.*

John's response was, "It may be a bad place to keep money, but how much do you have in your trash cans?" What John was saying was that the woman at least had the self-discipline to save in the first place.

In almost all cases, financial advisors recommend real estate as an effective way of accumulating wealth. Twenty years ago, financial planner Dennis Renter was able to put $3,000 down on a fixer-upper. He spent the next couple of years repairing it and increasing its value. He sold that house for $50,000 and then went on to buy another house for $100,000. He bought up like this five more times until he was able to purchase a $300,000 house. That house is now worth more than a million dollars and its value is still rising.

Financial planners understand that most people lack the discipline to make continuous investments into a financial plan. This is another reason owning a home can be such a good idea. Homes usually increase in value and owners must make payments or become homeless, so owning a home is sort of a forced wealth-accumulation program. The benefit is that the house, in most cases, goes up in value.

You can also develop your own discipline program by building it into the behavioral contract you established in Chapter Six. Let's say that you want to save enough money to buy an apartment complex as an investment. If you could come up with $50,000 you'd be set. Unfortunately, even though you and your spouse make a lot of money, neither of you has the discipline to save it.

Using your behavioral contract, you could outline an agreement stipulating that if you put fifteen percent of your gross income away every two weeks, you'll get to dine at the restaurant of your choice. Of course, to be most effective, the dinner should occur on the day that you actually put the money in question away for investment. Also, you may not want to choose a restaurant that will cost as much as the money you are trying to put away.

Will this work? You bet. If you involve your spouse with this strategy, you'll probably both have a list of restaurants picked out six weeks in advance.

The point is, building wealth doesn't have to be difficult. You just need to avoid setbacks and to develop a habit of saving and investing wisely. Conservative, slow investments have always been the best way to accumulate wealth.

4. **Review progress from investments every three months.** Monitor them, be aware of them, but under no circumstances should you change anything for at least two to three years following your initial decision to invest. The people who get in and out of investments quickly are usually those who suffer the most. To resist this temptation to change with the winds, use that technique we call attachment or anchoring and re-access the picture of your outcome in your mind. Have you got it? Now, at the height of

seeing, hearing, and feeling this emotion touch yourself on the arm or shoulder or even forehead to anchor that outcome in your mind. Now try to access the outcome again, but this time touch the same place you did before.

Remember this technique whenever you feel tempted to make a change in your investments, which can occur not only when you are tempted by a sexier-looking possibility but also when you get bored waiting for slow-growing investments to pay off.

5. **Diversify assets.** Good investors diversify. It's as simple as that. If you're invested in mutual funds, for example, invest in different sectors as hedges against a very cyclical economy and financial markets. Mutual funds come in very different styles, colors, and textures. They may consist of growth funds for example. These can increase in value very rapidly, especially when there is a lot of investment in newer technologies. During tougher economic times, you will be glad you invested in bond funds since they tend to move the opposite of the economy and thus are much more stable when the stock market is down. Or you may invest in value funds, which are more buoyant in volatile economies such as the one experienced in 2000–2001. If a financial portfolio consists only of real estate or bond funds, it could be negatively affected if the stock market rallies. Likewise, if you invest only in real estate and suddenly interest rates go up and buyer demand goes down, you could actually lose money, as many homeowners saw in the late 1980s and early 1990s. But if you are well diversified and invested in many sectors and asset classes, you will be able to weather nearly any economic downturn in any one area. This is sort of the investment metaphor of being careful not to put all your eggs in one basket.

And don't forget the magic of compound interest. Financial experts say that if you have the discipline to put $10,000 annually into a mutual fund that pays fifteen to eighteen percent interest, compound interest will net you more than 1.2 million dollars in twenty-eight years. You will make an enormous return on your money even if all you do is put the money in a savings account and leave it there. In fact, if you simply add $3,000 a year, you'll be a millionaire within twelve years. That's a goal many of us could achieve simply and easily.

> *The only thing important in the final hours of one's life isn't the money or the conquests; it's the people.*

You might be wondering if you have to be financially disciplined for the rest of your life. If opportunities to make a quick buck on a sure thing arise, should you take advantage of them? As far as I'm concerned, even surefire opportunities should be approached with discipline. After all, wanting money now is the reason many people make bad investments and lose money.

But . . . and this is a *big* but . . . do not make the same mistake Sam Walton of Wal-Mart fame and countless others have made: On his deathbed, Walton stated that he had blown it. The employee listening to Walton's last statements thought he was about to hear the CEO admit a scandal or, worse yet, a financial goal that had gone unrealized. Instead, Walton said he had blown it with his family. He'd spent so much time working, he barely knew his youngest son. His wife had stayed with him out of commitment. He had even neglected his grandchildren.

The only thing important in the final hours of one's life isn't the money or the conquests; it's the people. No one in the last stages of life ever looked back and regretted not making more money. It is always the relationships with loved ones they missed the most.

With that cautionary word duly noted, know that self-discipline will pay out for you in all areas of your life, and where wealth building is concerned, in the most tangible of ways: Self-discipline will give you the money to help you do exactly what you want with your life.

ASSIGNMENTS
Putting Self-Discipline to Work

1. Examine your belief system to see how wealth is represented in your mind. If you see doubt that you'll be able to stay on a financially self-disciplined plan, weaken that doubt and replace it with the belief that you have the power to handle great wealth, then use self-discipline to get it.
2. If you don't currently have an investment plan, take the first step in establishing one today. Pinpoint your outcomes. Find a professional to help you plan and invest. Find out what your net worth is, then think about the assets you'll utilize to work towards your outcomes. Then use your plan to see, hear, and feel what it will be like to achieve your goal.

SECRET
ten

Building Self-Discipline in Your Kids

> *There's nothing wrong with teenagers that reasoning with them won't aggravate.*
>
> Anonymous

There was once a little boy who had a bad temper. His father gave him a bag of nails and told him that every time he lost his temper, he must hammer a nail into the back of the fence.

The first day the boy drove thirty-seven nails into the fence. Over the next few weeks, as he learned to control his anger, the number of nails hammered daily gradually dwindled down. He discovered it was easier to hold his temper than to drive those nails into the fence.

Finally the day came when the boy didn't lose his temper at all. He told his father, who suggested that the boy now pull out one nail for each day that he was able to hold his temper. The days passed and the young boy was finally able to tell his father that all the nails were gone.

The father took his son by the hand and led him to the fence. He said, "You have done well, my son, but look at the holes in the fence. It will never be the same. When you say things in anger, they leave a scar just like this one. I'm proud that you have learned to control yourself, but remember: Every time you haven't, you've left a scar.

ANONYMOUS

Thanks to his father, this little boy learned his lesson, but almost everywhere you go these days you see kids who haven't: In malls, on airplanes, and even in the classroom, children are behaving as though there are no rules. Worse, they're getting away with it.

If a twelve-year-old shows disrespect for her parents, her bad behavior is dismissed as "Hormones kicking in." If a boy stays out three hours past curfew, his parents call it "One of those stages." If a wallet is stolen and a daughter says she didn't take it, her parents decide not to confront her even when they suspect she is the culprit.

Why are so many kids so ill behaved and undisciplined these days? Perhaps because we parents aren't teaching them otherwise.

The Age of Permissive Parents

Dr. Ruth Peters, a family therapist in Florida and author of the book *It's Never Too Soon*, blames many of kids' self-discipline problems on poor parenting. Her notion is that parents have raised a generation of kids who have never had to take no for an answer. She believes parents have become too tolerant, allowing children to make decisions that parents ought to make. She also maintains that mothers and fathers in two-income families feel increasingly guilty about spending so much time away from home. The result is, they feel unable to consistently apply stiff rules and regulations. What's more, they trade time with their kids for purchases in toy stores, handing out money in a guilt-ridden pseudo generosity that only serves to teach their children that if they ask long enough, they can get anything they want.

One typical mom in Dallas, Texas, worries that her four-year-old daughter doesn't have a traditional two-parent family. Debbie works full time and attends college in her spare moments. She is single, so Molly spends her day in childcare while Debbie worries that she may not be able to give Molly the material goods she deserves. Debbie tries to make up for her lack of time with Molly by giving her what she wants. For example, when Molly demands cookies for breakfast, Debbie complies. When Molly screams and throws tantrums, Debbie acquiesces instead of sticking by her rules. Her thought is that it just isn't worth it to fight with her. Yet Debbie is the first to say that it's important for Molly to learn she can't always get what she wants.

Make no mistake: Being consistent in disciplining your children and teaching them self-discipline when they are young are two of the most important factors involved in raising happy, healthy, respectful, and responsible kids. The fact is, when we try to give kids happier and more trouble-free lives, we take the struggle out of their lives and also the lessons they could learn in the process.

Besides, while setting behavioral limits and rules may be somewhat arbitrary, barriers for kids are not unfairly stifling. In fact, they are just the opposite. In a study done years ago on the effects of setting limits for kids, researchers found that without a fence, kids would stay in the center of a play area. When the play area was fenced, kids would venture out to the perimeter. This study wisely concluded that kids need self-discipline to feel secure enough to explore their surroundings.

Self-discipline builds in kids an understanding of themselves and a framework from which they can cope with life's difficulties, frustrations, and disappointments. Self-discipline also gives kids the tenacity and perseverance to focus on a job or task as long as is necessary to complete it. In this way they are able to learn and perfect their abilities to become adults who also make achievement and growth a habit. They can't do this if Mom or Dad completes tasks for them or buys them whatever they want without having to earn it.

Unfortunately, like Debbie, most parents today are so overwhelmed by their work and family demands that they are just plain exhausted at the very time they need the most commitment to applying consistent discipline. The result is parents who try to protect, prepare, and soothe their young instead of allowing them to suffer the consequences of their behavior. The natural extension is that kids are allowed to do what they want when they want it. When children are able to take control, the results are predictable.

> *The result is parents who try to protect, prepare, and soothe their young instead of allowing them to suffer the consequences of their behavior.*

According to a study done by Public Agenda, a New York public research organization, children under the age of twenty-one are increasingly lacking in morality and ethics. The study, funded by Ronald McDonald House Charities and the Advertising Council, asserts that the biggest problem of youth today is an absence of such basics as honesty, self-discipline, and a work ethic. Probably no generation has ever thought the current crop of kids was as respectful and ethical as they were at the same age, but this new research provides a look at the fire behind the smoke.

The most interesting aspect of the research, according to author Steve Farkas, is that eighty-one percent of adults believe parenting today is harder than ever. But eighty-three percent acknowledge that being a kid is also tougher. Surprisingly, the study shows these adults don't believe time spent with kids is a factor in how moral and ethical they are, nor is race, age, economic, or parental status thought to be a factor.

Interestingly, many parents do consider the threat of legal action to be important. Who hasn't heard reports of parents prosecuted under the statutes of child abuse for spanking their kids? My eight-year-old daughter once told me just before she was spanked for lying that I wasn't allowed to punish her in that fashion and that the police would arrest me if I did.

I just smiled and did the deed, but I couldn't help but wonder if she were right. Abuse is now defined as emotional trauma and threatening a child's welfare. What child doesn't feel emotional trauma during punishment? This feeling of government intrusion has an enormous influence on parents' perceptions of how they should—and can—raise their kids.

Moving Children towards Self-Discipline

Moving children towards self-discipline begins by assessing their abilities, skills, and emotional capabilities. You wouldn't expect a two-year-old to spend the day cleaning the toy room, but you could ask him to help you pick up, at first by putting only a few toys away, then more the next time. At age ten, you might ask him to pick up his room and make his bed before school. Tough to enforce? Yes, if you try to initiate the task all at once. But if you have expected your child to clean his room daily and have consistently enforced that request, it is as easy as making breakfast.

In my household, daughters Catherine and Caroline have always been responsible for cleaning up before they move onto another play activity, but it takes daily consistency on our part to enforce this. You can't enforce your rules once or twice a week and expect your child to be self-disciplined the rest of the month. One harried single mother recently told me that she is tired at the end of the day and the last thing she wants is to create conflict with her kids, especially when she hasn't seen them all day. She just wants to enjoy them. I asked, was she trying to be a parent or was she using her kids for entertainment? She appropriately thought I was abrupt, but I made my point.

> *You can't enforce your rules once or twice a week and expect your child to be self-disciplined the rest of the month.*

You don't need to feel that you can't enjoy time with your kids if you make rules and enforce them. A lot can be accomplished by the attitude you set. Yelling at your kids because they fail to clean a room in a timely manner will cause stress for everyone, but allowing your kids to do what they want will create more problems for them as adults. Playing with children and joking with them as you all clean the room together is the type of work/play kids love. I remember when Catherine was ten, all she wanted to do was play chase in the house. I negotiated with her that I would play hide and go seek three times, but after that she had to clean her room.

Who cares if your kids receive a treat before they begin their chores? Lighten up. They are only kids. Make work fun for them, especially when you first set rules. Later they won't dread living by them.

The Importance of Praise

You can also move children towards self-discipline by praising them. While praise has been shown to be the most valuable currency in increasing business productivity, ranking even higher than money in the minds of staff, it is even more effectively used in developing self-discipline in kids, both when they're small and when they're teens.

Praise works to build your child's self-esteem while encouraging the behavior you would like to see repeated. Praising your child is more fun than reprimanding him, but both are necessary. If you are doing it right, you will praise substantially more than you correct. Think of your child's self-worth level like a bank account. If you constantly make withdrawals with corrections and/or criticisms, the balance will be low. When it gets to zero, your child will act out with tantrums, yelling, aggression, and a myriad of other symptoms. But if your child's emotional bank account has frequent deposits of praise and acceptance and love, your child's sense of security will be strong, allowing him to stay disciplined in the tasks he attempts.

> *Praise works to build your child's self-esteem while encouraging the behavior you would like to see repeated.*

There is a place for negative punishment, of course. If your child were to run in the street chasing a ball, you would yell and scream instead of kindly asking that he not do it again. Such situations demand an immediate and strong response. Negative punishments work well, but they're also a painful experience to be reserved for only the most crucial situations.

At a mall recently, I followed a young mother with her ten-year-old son. He obviously didn't want to be there and kept drifting off behind her. Exasperated, she yelled at him to keep up by saying, "Why do I always have to ask you twice to do things? Why can't you be like your sister and just do the things I tell you to do?" Such harping causes a child not only to resent the parent but also to think that he can't succeed because he isn't good enough.

Parenting is one percent knowledge and ninety-nine percent patience. After you have asked your child for the fifth time to clean her room and she still doesn't do it, you are totally justified to yell and scream, but totally wrong to do it. Your child needs you to build her self-esteem and self-worth. In that way she can eventually build it herself. The way you discipline is a demonstration of how much worth children hold in your eyes.

You may be thinking that your kids don't do anything worth praising. Don't wait for them to do something right! Catch them in the act of doing something *close* to being right and praise them into being more disciplined.

Successive Approximation

This technique of praising kids when they are close to doing something you want is called successive approximation. Not only is it easy to implement, it works with small children as well as teens. Instead of waiting for your kids to do something perfectly, praise them for just starting a job. A kind word, a hand on the shoulder, a smile, and a hug are all techniques you can use to praise your kids. Not only are these effective, they are the best ways to praise your kids into doing what is right.

> *Parenting is one percent knowledge and ninety-nine percent patience.*

I recently asked my girls to take turns doing the dishes after dinner. The idea was to get them to alternate with one doing the dishes one week and the other the next. The problem is, they often forget. A gentle reminder usually does the trick, but a big gush of praise as they start toward the kitchen works even better. This technique works in stages.

Once she knew what was expected of her, I praised eight-year-old Caroline for merely taking the dishes off the table. The next day, I praised her only when she scraped the food into the compacter. The following day, I praised her only when she reached the rinsing stage. The threshold for receiving praise was low at first; she gradually had to do more to get praise and approval. At the end of the week, she received praise only when she did a good job from start to finish.

The objective is to create in children an inner reward, a type of self-praise that is reflected later in life as self-esteem. I can't be there to praise Caroline as an adult. It is important that if she takes on a task, she eventually feels that just doing it right is a way of feeling good about herself.

> *The objective is to create in children an inner reward, a type of self-praise that is reflected later in life as self-esteem.*

Here is a list of praise phrases you can use to build self-discipline in your child:

> You did a great job on that.
> Tell me how you did so well.
> I can see how hard you worked on this.
> You must feel very proud.
> I'd like to try that too. I hope I can do as good a job as you.
> You have put a lot of thought into this.

You can create more appropriate phrases than these, of course. The idea is to catch your child in the act of doing something right. Using successive approximation will create in them a desire for completion and a tenacity to strive even when they feel like giving up.

The Importance of Touch

Researchers at the University of Minnesota discovered years ago that humans can be persuaded not only by praise but also by touch and that the two together can be used to create a memory that will last a lifetime. To test the power of touch, two researchers left a quarter in a public phone booth. This was before the days of mobile phones, when the only way to make a call was to find a booth on a street corner. The researchers would wait for someone to pick the quarter up from the ledge and walk out, then one researcher would approach the individual and ask, "Did you find my quarter?" Only twenty-three percent of the culprits admitted taking the twenty-five cents.

> *People remember ideas longer when they are touched as they are spoken to.*

On another day, the researchers touched the stranger on the arm below the elbow, asking the same question, "Did you find my quarter?" In this case, eighty-three percent of the phone booth users returned the quarter. The researchers concluded that the participants were more persuaded when touch was involved.

In other studies on the power of touch, researchers have shown that people remember ideas longer when they are touched as they are spoken to.

I tried this concept in a restaurant many years ago. After speaking to the national restaurant association, I asked one manager to allow me to train his servers in an effort to increase tips. He was thrilled that I would be willing to help but he admitted that only great service could increase the size of tips. I told him that wasn't true. It was merely the perception of great service that would increase tips.

I taught his servers to touch the likely bill payer on the arm as they gave them the check with the comment, "I have really enjoyed serving you. Please come again soon." Other servers were asked to just use the words, "I have really enjoyed serving you. Please come again soon" without the touch.

The servers using the words and the touch together increased tips 150 percent. Customers were also asked after their meal what they thought of their server. The ones who received the touch were significantly happier with their service than the customers who weren't touched.

Such research speaks volumes about how you should praise your kids. If you would like your children to remember your praises longer and be more accepting of them, touch them as you make comments you want them to retain. Authors Spencer Johnson and Ken Blanchard pioneered this concept in their book *The One Minute Manager*.

Three-Step Praise

What I call the "three-step praise" works like this: First, praise your children in front of others. This will build them up in front of their friends as well as potentially cause their siblings to desire the praise as well.

The next step is to praise your child specifically for the behavior you want to encourage. Say, "You did a great job picking up sticks and raking the yard and thanks so much for doing it on the first request." As you say this, touch your child on the arm or shoulder to reinforce the comment.

Last, tell your child how proud you are of him and how well he is doing. Your child needs to associate approval with compliance with your rules and requests. When you make this association and it feels good to your child, he will make the same association when he needs to complete a project, even though he wants to go to bed or even when his friends are waiting for him to go out to play.

When my daughter Catherine was ten years old, I asked her to take out the recyclable drink cans and papers whenever she saw them accumulate. The first day she ignored the job.

The second day I reminded her. Later that day, she opened the door to look at the papers and cans. I saw her do it and praised her by saying, "Thanks Catherine for remembering to take out the recyclables" even though she hadn't so much as lifted one can off the ground. But she did sort of grimace a "Sure" and took them out. I wouldn't have cared at that point if she had picked up a single can or not. I was only concerned with using successive approximation in order to praise her for almost doing what I wanted.

The next day I reminded her again, but I praised her only when she took a bottle out to the recycler. The following day, she totally forgot the chore and I did not remind her, thinking she needed to remember it on her own.

The next day I asked her to come out to the garage out of earshot from her friend who was over for the day. I told her that she wasn't doing her chore and that I wanted her to do the job without me asking. She told me on the spot that she couldn't do it right then and it had to wait until her friend left. I repeated my reprimand more assertively but without yelling. I then touched her and said that she was doing a great job with all her other chores and how proud I was of her for the responsibility she was taking on and how well she was handling it. Catherine smiled and said, "Sure" again. But this time her smile was one of pride instead of inconvenience.

My daughter Caroline was a little more challenging. She is the one who will often run to Mom if she suspects Dad is being too demanding. I asked her to do the dishes for the rest of one week to which she complained that she was made to do all the work while her sister got off Scot-free. She also mentioned how unfair I was. I assertively reaffirmed my request while Caroline scowled but acquiesced. The next evening, she took her dishes to the sink but nothing else. I seized the opportunity to do the three-step praise. I touched her and loudly said, "Great job, Caroline. You remembered to do the dishes tonight." I then said, "I am very proud of you." Her sister Catherine then chimed in, "But Dad, she didn't do anything yet." I put my finger up to my mouth, hoping Catherine would take the hint and be quiet. Thankfully, Caroline ignored her sister and smiled at me nonetheless.

Three-Step Reprimand

The other part of the formula is what I call the "three-step reprimand." The first step is to get your child alone. If you embarrass him in front of his friends or siblings, he will try to sabotage your authority behind your back.

Next, be very specific with your reprimand. Never criticize your child by saying, "Why can't you mind me!" or "What did I just ask you to do?" This is so non-specific it creates anxiety. Instead, talk in a soft voice and tell him specifically what he did wrong, such as, "Sweetheart, I have asked you three times to sweep the garage and put away the tools. I won't ask again. I need you to do it now."

Last, touch your child on the arm or shoulders and tell him how great a job he always does and how proud of him you are. You will often get excuses as to why he can't obey. Just restate your reprimand and ask him again in a loving voice. This may not be your natural response. What you may really feel like doing is grabbing a wooden spoon and yelling, "If I have to ask again, I'm going to tan your hide!" But resist your anger and instead become lovingly assertive. Showing anger with your kids is really an admission that you don't have enough alternatives to deal with the situation.

> *Correct the behavior, praise the child.*

Also remember to separate the behavior you want to correct from the child's sense of self-worth. Always remember this phrase: Correct the behavior, praise the child. The more consistent you are with this technique, the more you can modify your child's behavior and build self-esteem. If you correct the behavior while praising the child, he will remember the correction while still feeling good about you and the reprimand. When children feel good about their self-worth, they are also prepared to sacrifice to do what they think is right, even when others tell them it's not worth it.

You won't always have to use the three-step praise or reprimand for every occurrence of success or disobedience. In fact, kids need to learn there won't always be someone there to tell them how great they have done or to correct them every time there is an infraction. But in the beginning you need to set patterns of success if you want your kids to develop self-discipline. To achieve a pattern of success, get in the habit of praising your kids three to five times each day. Use both the three-step praise and reprimand. Catch your children in the act of doing things right and correct them lovingly for those behaviors you want to change.

> *Get in the habit of praising your kids three to five times each day.*

Do this when your children are young and you will have children who accept correction instead of ones who reject and resent you for giving it. If you begin this when your children are teens, they will criticize and maybe even reject you, but if you start today and stay consistent, you will soon begin to have an impact on their behavior as well.

Be warned, though: If you get lazy and reprimand more than you praise, your kids will feel manipulated. Also, you will eventually be tempted to skip the reprimand and just yell because you are angry. Or you may be tempted to skip the three-step praise when you lack the time to do the whole process. If you let this happen, you will be in the same fix you were in before with your kids. You can't teach your kids discipline if you are not disciplined yourself.

The key is to get kids to engage and do things right because they want to and not to please someone else. This means raising kids in a way that causes them to feel good about actions and behaviors that utilize self-discipline.

Be a Good Model

If you tell your three-year-old not to hit the dog but you give old Rascal a good swat when he steals a piece of bread from the table, you're doomed. Likewise, if you tell your teen to put her clothes away but leave your own clothes lying around the living room, you're setting yourself up for disaster: Every child, every teen will pounce on a parent who hypocritically asks her to do something yet doesn't do it himself. This is because everything you say and do is a lesson to your kids.

The flip side is also true. Everything you neglect to say or do is also a lesson. All children learn by mirroring and copying. What your kids see and hear is also how they will think and behave. There is a point as teens mature when they seem to completely reject everything about their parents, but even though they won't admit it they continue to model your behavior. Consequently, your kids need to see you as a role model, not a friend. They have enough friends. They need parents who care enough about them to make sure they possess character, values, and morals and the only way they can learn this is to see those attributes in you.

Consider this scenario: Your kids are fighting in the back seat as you drive them to the park to play. You tell them that if they don't stop fighting, you will turn the car around and take them home. They are quiet for a while yet soon start fighting again. You tell them again to stop and the cycle repeats.

What your kids see and hear is also how they will think and behave.

What have they learned? To be quiet for thirty seconds while you calm down? More important, that you don't care enough about their behavior or your warning to follow through on it?

In another example, say a teacher tells a student that if she doesn't bring her grades up, she will be kicked off the cheerleading squad. The girl studies hard for a day and then goes back to the same habits that jeopardized her cheerleading activity in the first place. When she is eventually dismissed from the squad, she is outraged, claiming that the teacher is unfair and biased against her. Her parents take her side, blaming the teacher and the school instead of making the student accountable for her actions.

It doesn't end there. Years later, a boss tells her subordinate, the former cheerleader, to come to work on time instead of continuing to be chronically late. The employee apologizes and promises to be prompt the next day at 8:30 A.M. But at 7:30 A.M. she decides to spend extra time doing her hair and waits until the last minute to make the trek to work. There is an accident on the road and she is again late.

Wouldn't a disciplined worker leave twenty minutes ahead of time, making sure she arrived on schedule? Responsibility is a lesson she should have learned as a child, because a child who is required to consistently clean her room, earn decent grades, and complete her chores knows how to take responsibility for her behavior as an adult.

The Nitty-Gritty of Teaching Young Children Self-Discipline

Ah, young children. They require a lot of attention. After all, some of them hit. Some of them have temper tantrums. Some take things that don't belong to them. Some perpetually steal toys from their siblings. Some will perpetually scale any barrier and get into what they're not supposed to. The list could go on forever! For obvious reasons, not the least of which is keeping parents sane, it's wise to start teaching children self-discipline when they're young. One of the most effective ways of doing this is to use time-outs.

Time-Outs

Say your child throws a tantrum in front of company. You are angry. But instead of paddling him in front of your friends, you give four-year-old Jessica a time-out.

Experts prescribe time-outs as a way for children to think about their actions and what they did wrong, but they serve an even better purpose: Time-outs give the child a chance to gain self-control. A child who is out of control is irrational and unable to make a clear assessment of his options. A child who is in control is able to evaluate the best way to handle a situation.

You tell young Tyler that you would like him to pick up his toys. At five years of age, he sees that request on par with writing *War and Peace* in an afternoon. It is impossible and after a few half-hearted minutes of picking up his cars, he breaks down crying and screaming. What do you do? Hold him and tell him he doesn't have to pick up? That you will do it instead? Or immediately give him a time-out and talk to him again when he is in control?

Your child's behavioral breakdowns are designed to test your resolve. Are you willing to allow your child to control the situation or are you willing to be tough and follow through with your instructions?

When she was seven years old, Caroline started to scream one morning after I told her to clean her room. I left for work and told her to have it done by the time I arrived home for dinner. When I returned, her room was still in shambles. She wanted to watch a TV program after dinner and started to throw a tantrum when I asked her to clean her room instead. I told her to go to her room for a time-out. She said, "Good, I don't have to clean my room now." I ignored her remark and waited for seven minutes.

> *Time-outs give the child a chance to gain self-control.*

After the punishment, I walked into her room and told her that just because she had received a time-out didn't mean she was released from obeying my request. She cried again. But this time, she realized that getting a time-out and then also having to do the chore wasn't worth the inappropriate behavior that got her the time-out in the first place.

As the above examples make clear, time-outs can be tailored to the age of the child. Typically, experts recommend one minute for each year your child is old. Thus, a two-year-old would receive a two-minute time-out; a six-year-old would receive a six-minute time-out.

Withholding Privileges

As your child gets a little older, the technique of withholding privileges can be added to the arsenal of techniques parents have to teach self-discipline. For example, if in spite of the three-step-praise and three-step-reprimand seven-year-old Tony continues to kick his younger brother or the dog whenever he's frustrated, he can systematically lose all the privileges he enjoys. When the hour comes when he's not allowed to watch TV, to go outside, to play with his trucks, or to play with friends, he will have ample time to reflect on the reason why—and to take to heart the necessity of stopping the undesirable behavior.

Parents must merely be willing to make their children temporarily unhappy and to communicate to them beforehand what is expected and what will happen to them if those expectations are not met. You are showing your children mercy or empathy by saving them from consequences, but you are only teaching them that there are no repercussions when they don't take responsibility for their actions. Withholding consequences isn't what will happen when they are out in the "real world," and you are not helping them prepare for this world by withholding consequences now.

You may be thinking that it is too harsh to hold children to the same consequences adults must submit to. You are right. But you can simulate consequences that children can identify with. If your child breaks another's toy, they can be made to pay for half of it. If your child is late to school or a function, you can take TV time away. The better you can prepare your children for adulthood, the more mature and well adjusted they will be when they get there.

Teaching Teens Self-Discipline

Teen are a slightly different beast than young children and, without a doubt, can be more challenging. All around them are temptations such as skipping school, shoplifting, cheating on tests, or engaging in sexual, drug, or alcohol-related activities. Consequently, teens need self-discipline today more than ever. The reason they are so difficult to control? Two words: "Peer pressure."

There are two main reasons why teens cave into peer pressure:

1. **They want to act like adults in a group they respect.** Often teens will do anything to gain entry to this group, even engage in an activity they know is wrong, because their peers are hip and their parents are embarrassing.

   Ironically, a large part of helping your child deal with a desire to prematurely separate from parents is to simply spend more time with them. When my niece Kelly was thirteen, she went from a quiet angel to a raging hormonal emotional slicer and dicer. My brother Kevin took her skiing to Snowbird, Utah, and Kelly complained and whined the whole time. But as it turned out, from the ashes of discomfort came a Phoenix of stability. Kevin soon after became coach of her basketball team. He then took a

   > *Ironically, a large part of helping your child deal with a desire to prematurely separate from parents is to simply spend more time with them.*

job as coach of her volleyball team and Kelly has completely turned around.

I went through a messy divorce in 1988. The lawyer on the other side made the statement that I didn't deserve joint custody of my daughter Stacey other than every other weekend. After all, quality time is better than quantity time, isn't it?

Research has now shown the opposite. Quantity time is what kids need. Quality is nice, but what they need most is for you to be there. Kids who see a parent only on weekends have many more self-discipline problems than those who have frequent contact. In fact, studies of same-sex marriages without fathers show that children crave a father for the boundaries he can contribute and the authority he can convey. Moms and dads each make a contribution toward the development of their kids. If one is absent, the child's development becomes lopsided.

2. **They are unable to stand up for their convictions**. Teens who give in to peer pressure may know something is wrong, but they don't have the courage to say no, especially when saying yes will gain them approval, attention, and love from their friends. For example, say a teenage boy is told by his friends that if he doesn't drink with the rest of the fellows, he's going to have to find someone else to hang out with. This boy doesn't want to drink and knows it's wrong, but he desperately wants to be a part of the group. Being lonely is no fun. In spite of his better judgment, he begins drinking with them, eventually drinking a lot with them, and when the group begins getting in trouble for their various drunken escapades, he's a part of it.

It is possible to build self-discipline in teens. The following ten-step method can help.

Ten-Step Method for Building Self-Discipline in Teens

1. **Allow your teen to take responsibility.** Teens are trying to become independent. Give them enough freedom to test their abilities. If they want to procrastinate working on a project until the night before it is due, let them. They will learn to give themselves more time to complete it on their next attempt, especially if you give them consequences for bad grades.

    It's tough to see kids go through setbacks, but that is what they are, setbacks and not failures. If you rescue your child without letting him learn from his errors, he will repeat them. It's a lot easier to allow your child to go to grade school without a show and tell article than it is for a senior in high school to miss a deadline on a major project or possibly even fail a grade because he wasn't held accountable. You won't always be there to rescue your child, so let him learn these important lessons early.

2. **Don't let the mosquitoes get you.** To a teen there are only major issues, no small ones. If parents decide to fight every battle, they will lose most. Decide which battles are the ones worth suiting up for. If your teen wants to change her hair color, don't make an issue about it. But if she wants to get a tattoo or pierce a body part, take your stand. If your teen wants to stay out until midnight with some friends, evaluate whether she can be trusted to come home on time. If she wants to go out with kids you know are bad, put your foot down.

3. **Make your teen a team player.** The antidote to resisting dangerous temptations is to give teens ever-increasing responsibilities consistent with their age and level of maturity. This helps kids develop character, morality, values, and self-discipline—the armor kids can wear

against emotional weakness. It allows them to say no when they believe something is wrong and helps them set boundaries. It helps them become assertive in dealing with peers. It allows them to raise their self-worth so they still have a desire to belong, but helps them stay away from bad kids and instead look for those who share constructive interests.

> *Character, morality, values, and self-discipline—the armor kids can wear against emotional weakness.*

It is easy to give up and let your teen do whatever he wants, especially if you are hassled over everything you ask him to do, but make sure your teen has responsibilities in your home that you hold him accountable to nonetheless. Those tasks can be anything from mowing the lawn to helping with the laundry. Yes, it is easier if you do it yourself, but it won't teach your teen responsibility. Make sure your teen knows he is contributing to the well being of the family.

4. **Take parenting seriously, not yourself**. You are not the best parent in the world and also not the worst. If you care, you can't permanently scar your kids. You also need to know that your kids don't want a prison guard for a parent. They want a counselor, often on demand, who counsels but doesn't control. Give your kids as many new experiences as you can but don't worry about what you are or aren't doing. If you need to be tough, tell your kids that your Mr. Hyde persona has taken the place of Dr. Jekyll. They will get the message. And remember to have fun with your kids. They will also get the message they shouldn't be so serious either.

My daughter Stacey once wanted me to appeal to her mother to allow her to go out even though she had violated curfew and had been told to stay home the next two weekends. Outraged at the consequence,

Stacey very sweetly and innocently asked if I would help. I told her that if it were left to me, I would take away her driving privileges as well. Stacey screamed, "You don't care about me. You don't love me and you have no idea what I need or want." She added, "I can't believe how mean you are. No other parent treats their kids as bad as you do."

I tried not to smile too visibly, though I wanted to laugh out loud. Instead I said, "I know sweetheart. I am so mean, sometimes I want to give myself a time-out." This didn't make Stacey feel any better, but it did keep me from becoming angry. One of the toughest phases for single parents to go through is dealing with an adolescent who screams at them and tells them they are the worst parent in the world. It's hard not to have the support of a partner in the home to back them up. You need to stay sane by keeping it light. Don't get angry, and remember, "This too shall pass."

> *You need to stay sane by keeping it light.*

5. **Build up trust**. There isn't a teen out there who doesn't think she deserves more trust from Mom and Dad. The problem is that little Jenny or young Tom has at one point or another done something to lose that trust. I recently told my daughter Catherine to clean her room before she called her friends to play. When I got home from work, her room was a mess and she was spending the night at a friend's house. I was irritated that she hadn't listened to me. So the next day I told her to clean her room and I watched her do it. She said, "Dad, why are you watching me?" I said, "Sweetheart, I want to make sure you do what I tell you to do." She said, "I can't do it if you watch me. You don't trust me to clean my own room?" I said, "Nope, you have lost my trust for today. But you can earn it back. In the meantime, there is no TV for the next week

until you clean your room first. Then we can start to talk about trust again."

If this seems a little harsh, consider your daughter as a teenager, staying out way past curfew, perhaps until 2:00 A.M. Imagine how you'd feel if she didn't call and she wasn't at the place she said she'd be. Deal with the issue of trust now and you won't have to cope later with the horrific worry of wondering if your kid is in trouble.

> *Deal with the issue of trust now and you won't have to cope later with the horrific worry of wondering if your kid is in trouble.*

Trust is so important that I recommend you test it frequently in the little things when your children are young. If they are trustworthy in the little things, they will be trustworthy in the big ones. If they lie to you about a small issue, treat it like it's a big one. As they get older, give them increasingly harsh consequences if they lie. If you can't trust your teen, you have opened them up to drug abuse, underage drinking, sex, and a myriad of other deep pits you want to keep them out of. But most important, you will have no choice but to communicate to them that they can't be trusted. Consequently, they will act in an untrustworthy fashion. Build up trust by making them faithful in small things first, and do it when they are young.

6. **Speak their language**. Teens have a short attention span when talking to adults. The last thing they want to hear is some diatribe about how to get better grades or why they need to dress more conservatively. Learn to speak their language by listening to the way they talk to their peers, then mirror those words. My daughter Catherine uses the word "whatever" to communicate that she is no longer wants to listen and at the same time disagrees. It's sort of a catchall phrase of displeasure. She pronounces the word as though it's two words, "Whatever," usually with disgust dripping from her voice.

Whenever she stalls doing her homework and offers excuses or complains about her sister, I just have to voice that one word, pronouncing it as she does, and she knows exactly what I mean.

When my other daughter wears something I think is inappropriate, I use just one word: "Change." Often I add please at the end, but you know what I mean. I don't explain my reasoning or justify it. If Caroline wants to discuss it more, I am willing to talk as long as it doesn't become the foundation for an argument. But I also don't want to give her any opportunities to challenge me either. One word does it.

If they are trustworthy in the little things, they will be trustworthy in the big ones.

7. **Expect good work**. The ethic of doing a good job starts in childhood and is cemented in adolescence so insist on high standards in whatever your teen does. It is easy for teens to do a halfway job just to get a task finished, especially when most parents won't evaluate it anyway. The problem is that teens will extend this lackadaisical effort to other tasks as well. A poor job cleaning the room that is accepted as complete extends to an equally poor job on a report that is due for science or English class. Expecting high standards of work now will install an ethic in your teen that will last long after they leave you for the adult world.

8. **Fade to black**. As time goes on, your job is to become less of an influence on your teen, not more. You are there to teach them how to make decisions, not make them yourself. You need to become less so they can become more. In the sitcom *Everybody Loves Raymond*, the family of the grown son moves in across the street and visits without warning nearly every day. The problem is the mother, a controlling woman who thinks her parenting duties extend throughout life. In one

episode, she brings over a cake and insists that Raymond eat it because he looks so skinny that day.

In a similar situation, a mother of a teen girl recently told me they do everything together, even talk about each other's boyfriends and gossip. That statement made me cringe. Her teen needs a parent who is there to help steer her toward success as an adult, not become her best childhood friend. It's important to be close to your kids, but not at the expense of being a parent. Friends don't direct or supervise another, nor do they enforce consequences. Friends accept one another without judgment, while a parent is there to judge and correct—exactly what teens need. One bright teen told a group of peers, "I love my mom; we're good friends. But I already have friends. I want a mom."

> *Expecting high standards of work now will install an ethic in your teen that will last long after they leave you for the adult world.*

9. **Make your teen feel loved, no matter what happens.** If you're not careful, arguments, fights, and disagreements can turn into feelings of anger and emotional abandonment. Kids frequently feel that if they don't have your approval, they don't have your love. It's important to communicate to them that you will always love them, no matter what happens. The more you tell them this, the more they will be able to resist peer pressure in their teen years. If you don't tell them, they may begin looking elsewhere for the love and affection they don't get from you.

10. **Be consistent. This is the most important part of building self-discipline in your teen.** Playing tough one day only to let your child slide the next is a nightmare of mixed signals. If you prepare your children for consistency as teens, they will expect consistency as adults. If you adopt a permissive stance in their teen years, they will expect the same later.

The fact remains that you are busy and don't always have a great deal of time to devote to your teen, but consider this scenario: Say a child is raised in a permissive home separated from responsibility and consequences and is taught that if he doesn't want to do his homework, Mom will talk to the teacher and get an extension. Or, if he doesn't want to go to school, Dad will call and get him a day off or write him an excuse.

As a teen, this boy fathers a child and denies it. After breaking a number of hearts, he marries shortly after college but divorces before he is twenty-five. He marries again and has two kids. He argues with his wife because of money and again initiates divorce, this time because he wants to marry someone more attractive. He sees his children on occasional weekends but never takes a strong role in their lives. They grow up angry and disillusioned and with numerous significant problems of their own. The man's new wife also disappoints him. After a third divorce, he marries for a fourth time in his fifties but soon divorces again due to "irreconcilable differences."

Excuses when they're children means unreliability when they're adults.

Does this actually happen? Yes, every day, all around you, to people you know. The divorce rate for first marriages today is sixty-two percent nationwide; seventy-eight percent for second marriages.

Commitment, duty, and faithfulness are not just Marine Corp slogans. You can teach these lessons to your kids. Start by consistently making them clean their rooms and complete their other chores. Make sure they treat adults with respect. Make sure they get their homework done on time.

Excuses when they're children means unreliability when they're adults. The more you let them slide as children, the tougher things will be fifteen years later. The best time for your child or teen to learn self-discipline is now.

ASSIGNMENTS
Putting Self-Discipline to Work

1. Set up three rules for your children that you care about enough to enforce consistently. Come up with consequences that are not harsh but instead are appropriate. Arriving at the dinner table upon the first request may be nice, but you may not care enough about it to exact a punishment or consequence if the rule is broken.

    My kids used to be frequently late for school in the morning, so we decided one of our rules was that they needed to be in the car by 8:15 every morning or they received no TV time that night. Ironically, the kids often didn't think about the consequence in the morning, but it really hit them when their favorite programs came on after diner and they were unable to watch them.

2. Begin using the three-step praise and three-step reprimand techniques on your kids today and praise them for doing things that are close to being right. Don't wait for them to perform perfectly—this may never happen. Build their self-esteem by praising them for being approximately right.

3. The next time your kids make mistakes, allow them to experience the consequences. If they lie, push them to apologize to the person they dishonored. If they steal, make them replace the article they stole with a similar but better item. If they break an object, make them replace it. Don't protect your kids from experiencing the consequences of their actions or they will be doomed to repeat the same mistakes over and over again.

SECRET
eleven

Self-Discipline and Your Spiritual Walk with God

> *Toward what should we aim if not toward God?*
>
> André Gide

A man was sleeping one night when suddenly his room filled with light and the Savior appeared. The Lord told the man He had work for him to do and showed him a large rock in front of his cabin. The Lord then explained that the man was to push against the rock with all his might.

This the man did, day after day. For many years, he toiled from sun up to sun down, his shoulders set squarely against the cold, massive surface of the unmoving rock, pushing with all his might. Each night the man returned home sore and worn out, feeling that his whole day had been spent in vain.

Finally, he went to the Lord with his troubles. "Lord," he said, "I have labored long and hard in Your service, putting all my strength to that which You have asked me. Yet after all this time, I have not budged the rock. What is wrong? Why am I failing?"

The Lord responded compassionately. "My friend, when I asked you to serve Me and you accepted, I told you your task was to push against the rock with all your strength. This you have done. Never once did I mention that I expected you to move the rock. Your task was to push. And now you come to Me with your strength spent, thinking that you have failed. But is that really so?

"Look at yourself. Your arms are strong and muscled, your back is sinewy and brown, your hands are callused, and your legs have become massive and hard. Through opposition you have grown much and your abilities now surpass that which you used to have. You haven't moved the rock, but your calling was to be obedient and to push and to exercise your faith and trust in My wisdom. This you have done.

"I, my friend, will now move the rock."

ANONYMOUS

In Biblical times, cities possessed defenses commensurate with the size of their walls. Archeologists report that the walls of the ancient city of Babylon, for example, were one hundred feet high and wide enough to race six chariots side by side. The city itself was eleven miles in circumference and virtually impregnable. With the Euphrates River flowing through it, it even had its own water source. There was no way an invader without gunpowder sufficient to knock down walls could have conquered it from without. Instead, it was taken from within.

The Medes and Persians joined forces and laid siege to the city. Belshazzar, the arrogant king of Babylon, was so confident of his fortifications that he threw a party despite the threat of invasion. Drunk, he didn't notice that Darius the Mede and the allied invaders had rerouted the Euphrates, leaving a passage for troops to enter. Babylon fell that night without a fight, though the city was so large it took three days for all its inhabitants to realize it had been taken.

Proverbs 25:28 says, "A man without self-control is as defenseless as a city with broken down walls." Babylon's walls weren't broken down in a literal sense, but in a metaphorical one they most certainly were.

Cities today may not need walls for protection, but how safe would you feel if you turned on CNN to see a report that the president of the United States had been persuaded to disarm the armed forces and was unilaterally removing all radar, early warning systems, and weapons and was even dismantling the CIA and national security agencies? Would you feel confident, even if he told the country not to worry, that other countries had promised to remove their weapons also?

> *"A man without self-control is as defenseless as a city with broken down walls."*

The Bible recognizes that a person without self-discipline is like any city or country without its defenses. Because we live in a world that contains evil, we need defenses. On an individual level, there is only one true defense against vice and sin and that is in using self-discipline to strengthen our spiritual walk with God and our understanding of God's word.

Being Obedient to God's Word

Have you ever prayed for God's will, no matter what it is? The only way to discover God's will is to be obedient to

God's word. As Psalms 110:9–11 asks, "How can [we] stay pure? By reading Your word and following its rules. I have tried my best to find You. Don't let me wander off from Your instructions. I have thought much about Your words and stored them in my heart so that they would hold me back from sin."

Proverbs 2:3–5 adds, "If you want better insight and discernment, and are searching for them as you would for lost money or hidden treasure, then wisdom will be given to you and knowledge of God Himself; you will soon learn the importance of reverence for the Lord and of trusting Him."

Gaining Wisdom

This wisdom is essential if we're going to be obedient to God's word. The tough part is remembering that wisdom also comes from making mistakes. A pastor once said that God gives us wisdom and thankfully doesn't always make us learn it on our own. True as this is, it's also true that often we make the same mistakes time and again.

> *God gives us wisdom and thankfully doesn't always make us learn it on our own.*

We all know that certain men are bad news, but rather than avoid them, some women allow themselves to repeatedly follow through on their attraction to this type of man. Without wisdom, we *all* make the same mistakes over and over.

Several years ago, I was in need of an administrative assistant/office manager. I hired a man who talked big but was undependable. I must admit I am attracted to people with a "can do" attitude. I really want to let capable people take the reins and run, but what I really needed was someone who was dependable and showed up for work. I needed someone who could get the job done day in and day out, no matter how boring the tasks were.

My smooth talking administrative assistant/office manager acted like he could solve all the problems he saw and could make my business run like a sewing machine. Unfortunately, he not only didn't get assignments done on time, he also convinced me that he was overburdened and needed help. I actually hired an assistant for him! Within one week, he had her running his personal errands, washing his car, and picking up his laundry. When I terminated him, I felt that this was a good lesson to learn, once. Then I made the same mistake again.

> *"If you have the faith of a mustard seed, you will be able to say to a mountain, 'Move,' and it will move. Nothing will be impossible to you."*

Attracted to the same bravado of "I can do anything and make the office sing with success," I hired another individual who talked a big game. The results were predictable. Within two weeks, my new employee had over-billed customers $80,000, resulting in at least $150,000 in lost business for my corporation.

Is it just me, or are many of us slow learners of wisdom? The sad truth is that without God's help and without His wisdom, we are forever doomed to repeating our mistakes.

With God's help and wisdom, we not only learn from our mistakes, God teaches us His word. In short, the way to gain wisdom is by following God's word and will as written in the Bible.

Keeping Faith

One of the most important things God tells us to do is to keep faith. Jesus Christ once said, "If you have the faith of a mustard seed, you will be able to say to a mountain, 'Move,' and it will move. Nothing will be impossible to you." In spite of these inspiring words, keeping faith isn't always easy.

Say your boss tells you to spend the weekend wining and dining a client. You have been traveling so much that your wife and kids hardly remember what you look like. You want a raise and promotion and know that you need to put in extra work to get them, yet God's word says that you must love your wife as Christ loved the church. Being away constantly does not show your love for your family. Do you put your faith in the hope that your boss will notice your hard work and reward you, or in God's word?

Keeping faith can be difficult, but as the following story illustrates, those who do so receive abundant blessings:

> A small congregation in the foothills of the Great Smoky Mountains had built a new sanctuary on a piece of land willed to them by a church member. Ten days before the new church was to open, the local building inspector informed the pastor that the parking lot was inadequate for the size of the building. Until the church doubled the size of the parking lot, they would not be able to use the new sanctuary.
>
> Unfortunately, the church with its undersized lot had used every inch of their land except for the mountain against which it had been built. In order to build more parking spaces, they would have to move the mountain out of the back yard.
>
> Undaunted, the pastor announced the next Sunday morning that he would meet that evening with all members who had "mountain moving faith." They would hold a prayer session asking God to remove the mountain from the back yard and to somehow provide enough money to have it paved and painted before the scheduled opening dedication service the following week.
>
> At the appointed time, twenty-four of the congregation's three hundred members assembled for prayer.

Self-Discipline and Your Spiritual Walk with God

They prayed for nearly three hours. At ten o'clock, the pastor said the final "Amen."

"We'll open next Sunday as scheduled," he assured everyone. "God has never let us down before and I believe He will be faithful this time too."

The next morning as the pastor was working in his study there came a loud knock at his door. When he called "Come in," a rough looking construction foreman appeared, removing his hard hat as he entered.

"Excuse me, Reverend. I'm from Acme Construction Company over in the next county. We're building a new shopping mall over there and we need some fill dirt. Would you be willing to sell us a chunk of that mountain behind the church? We'll pay you for the dirt we remove and pave all the exposed area free of charge, if we can have it right away. We can't do anything else until we get the dirt in and allow it to settle properly."

The little church was dedicated the next Sunday as originally planned and there were far more members with "mountain moving faith" on opening Sunday than there had been the previous week!

Anonymous

Can you apply the concept of "keeping faith" to the various relationships you have? Look at your marriage. Perhaps all the fizz has gone out of it. You and your husband are indifferent to one another, your friends tell you to leave him, and you know you are attractive to co-workers. Maybe divorce is an option. You don't have kids, so except for your marital vows there really isn't any bond to keep you together.

But the Bible says that God hates divorce, though He allows divorce when adultery has taken place. What should you do? It's no longer fun being married, but you made a commitment. You just never knew marriage would be this hard. Following God's will by staying married, working to improve your marriage, and having faith that this is the right decision is tough.

Romans 8:28 reports that, "All things work for good for those who love the Lord and are called according to His will." The critical part of this passage is "called according to His will." This does not mean that all things will work out well, but if you seek God's will for your life, all things work out for good.

I was counseling a woman a few years ago whose son was deeply rebellious. He was taking drugs and stealing to maintain his habit. The woman made a surprising comment. She said, "The Bible says all things work out for good, so I really shouldn't worry." But the opposite was true. She really did need to worry about her son. She needed to get him back home and better supervised. Even though the word of God promises that our faith will be rewarded, we still have responsibilities to our children. The Bible commands parents to train a child up in the way that is pleasing to God. This means we have to use common sense and to act with the wisdom God has given us when our children behave in ways that are not pleasing to God—or to us.

> "All things work for good for those who love the Lord and are called according to His will."

As previously hinted, one of the most important areas in which we need to keep faith and be obedient to God's word involves choosing a mate. God told Adam in the beginning that it was not good for him to be alone, that he needed a helpmate. God also said it's important to be equally yoked with a believer who shares the same faith as you.

The idea is that if you are unequally yoked, as an ox might be unequally yoked with another in tilling a field, the cultivation will be unbalanced. In the field, the plow will sink deeper on one side than the other. In a marriage,

Self-Discipline and Your Spiritual Walk with God

unequally yoked individuals will fight with one another and encounter constant conflict.

God thus instructs us to marry another believer, to become equally yoked and balanced, yet this takes enormous self-discipline. In the heat of attraction, it's not easy to stop and contemplate whether the person you are attracted to is spiritually right for you.

Perhaps you meet someone who is great looking, kind, intelligent, articulate, and educated. The only problem is, he doesn't believe in God. But he loves you and wants to marry you. How can you reject him? You are in love and you marry, even though you are unequally yoked. As the years go by, your partner lives according to what he thinks is right, not what God wants. After years of marriage, you beg this person to go to church with you but he never does. He resents that you attend church as well. The last straw comes when you discover your perfect mate has cheated on you.

> *God thus instructs us to become equally yoked and balanced.*

Would you have had so many problems had you married a Christian and been equally yoked? The answer is, you both would have turned to God's word sooner. Many of your problems never would have existed because you would have been in prayer as a couple and as a family staying closer to what God wanted. Christians aren't perfect, just forgiven. The issue beckons back to that first undisciplined decision to marry. God said, marry another believer. Be equally yoked with another.

Keeping Our Children Safe

We need to be obedient to God's word in other areas, too. It's frequently observed that teens today encounter almost unbearable peer pressure. Say your teen is a freshman in college. There is alcohol all around him and nonstop parties every night. The resident assistants try to keep things under control, but they're only a few years older than your child. What is there to stop kids from self-destructing when binge drinking is the norm, not the exception, on nearly all major campuses?

There's God. Proverbs 22:6 says, "Train a child up in the way he should go and when he is old he will not depart from it." Morality isn't just what you and I think about how we should conduct ourselves in life. Morality is a God-given code that will help our kids successfully and productively move through life. Many people self-destruct because they are drawn to excess and temptation. Who among us doesn't know of someone who partied too much and didn't make it through college, or someone who wasn't able to spend the time necessary to become successful in her career, or worse yet, someone who didn't spend enough time with his kids and watched his family grow further and further apart? Discipline yourself in everything you do, especially in the way you walk with the Lord.

> Date rape is so prevalent now that twenty-five percent of women will be raped at some time in their lives.

Of course, alcohol isn't the only thing teens need to worry about. Date rape is so prevalent now that twenty-five percent of women will be raped at some time in their lives, many of them on college campuses. But there is also another side to the epidemic of rape and that is the alarming claim of false reports of rape. The Baltimore Raven football team recently employed a lawyer to conduct a seminar warning the players of women who will report rape even though sex is consensual. It is often the word of a seemingly defenseless rape victim against that of a big, brawny, often unsuspecting player. It may be hard to side with an often promiscuous and highly paid football player but even they are sometimes falsely accused. The problem is that players have been accused of rape so often that many people automatically assume they are guilty without hearing the facts. Certain women play on that assumption, often netting large monetary settlements without having to prove a rape was committed.

During the seminar, the lawyer told the players the best way to protect themselves was to stop having casual sex. The players laughed nervously at that unrealistic prospect. The bottom line is that if the players were more disciplined in the first place, they would not be in positions that could lead to prison or substantial monetary settlements. In short, many players are condemned to trouble because they are ignoring God's word regarding casual sex.

Our youngest children are also becoming immune to the effects of vice and immorality in the media. TV, movies, print, and other sources inevitably portray aberrant sexual behavior as normal. On vacation recently in the state of Washington, my two daughters were watching TV. At home in California, my wife and I heavily screen the programs they watch. They are allowed to view cartoon channels, Christian broadcasts, and videos we purchase for them. At the vacation house, a family heirloom built by my wife's grandfather in 1910, the house wasn't hooked up with cable so only three stations were available on the antenna: Fox, CBS, and ABC. My daughters, eight and ten years old, first watched a Fox sitcom at 9:00 P.M. This show portrayed a woman coaxing an acquaintance to sleep with her. I turned the channel to find a reality TV show on CBS using words even my sports friends wouldn't voice in the locker room. ABC wasn't much better. It was re-broadcasting a mafia movie showing a priest seducing a woman he was counseling.

It hit me suddenly that this was the world's way of lowering our defenses, just as Solomon mentioned in the quote from Proverbs 25:28: "A man without self-control is as defenseless as a city with broken down walls." After a period of years of lowered defenses, there are none left.

The results are predictable: Underage drinking occurs because kids see people using alcohol or even drunk on TV nightly. Teen pregnancies occur because kids see sex many times a day on TV and think there is no prohibition against it.

Though we live in the fleshly desires of our appetites and lusts, what really controls us is the spirit. That control is either of God or Satan, and Satan has control until we accept Jesus Christ into our hearts and lives. To put it another way, I once heard that we humans are like a house. Either Satan is the occupant or God is, but they can't both be residents at the same time.

During Christ's walk on the earth, He came upon a man who was possessed by demons. When Christ cast the demons out, the Pharisees, the spiritual leaders of the day, wondered if the power to cast out demons was Satanic. Jesus, indignant at the remark, told them that Satan wouldn't cast out his own.

Using self-discipline in line with God's word will help you grow and develop in God's plan for your life.

But applying only self-discipline against Satan's influence won't work. It must be the power of God that makes change in your life. Using self-discipline in line with God's word will help you grow and develop in God's plan for your life.

Praying for God's Blessings in Your Life

This brings us to prayer. While over eighty-five percent of Americans believe in the power of prayer, most admit they don't take sufficient time to do it. James 5:16 says, "Confess your sins to each other and pray for each other so that you may be healed. The earnest prayer of a righteous person has great power and wonderful results."

One of the central tenets of a spiritual walk is prayer. It is literally a telephone call to the presence of God. The Lord tells us that prayer is like the sweet smell of incense to Him. God hears prayer and wants us to pray and give all our troubles to Him. Indeed, the New Testament of the Bible tells us to pray without ceasing, while Psalms 65:2 says, "O God of Zion, we wait before You in silent praise, and thus fulfill our vow. And because You answer prayer, all mankind will come to You with their requests."

One of the ways you can be assured your faith is strong is that you experience God's answers to prayer, but often God takes His time providing those answers. What's more, God doesn't give us everything we want because many of our requests aren't the best things for us or even good for us. A phrase that explains this goes, "Waiting on the Lord." When we pray, we wait on God to give us answers and solve our problems. When we pray, we are telling God we need His help. When we pray for God's will for our lives, we are asking for God's best for us instead of what the child in us wants right now.

When we pray for God's will for our lives, we are asking for God's best for us instead of what the child in us wants right now.

Just think what would happen if God gave us everything we wanted! Would it make us happy? The answer lies in considering the requests our kids make. When your four-year-old wants to eat cookies and ice cream for every meal, is it right to grant her requests? No. You provide nourishing meals because that is what is best for her.

I can only imagine the number of lottery players who pray to God each week to let them win. Some may even promise to share their winnings with God, as if He needs their help. But winning may be a terrible answer to prayer. Eighteen percent of California lottery millionaires have gone bankrupt within three years of winning, most with no history of credit problems. Were they better off before or after their great fortune? Great wealth may not be the best thing for you. It is much better to pray for God's will in your life, because God does want what is best for you.

It's also important to thank God for your blessings through prayer. I recently flew on Alaska Airlines on a business trip. Sixty years before, a CEO had left the airline to work as a missionary but before he left he saw to it that a legacy would be included on every flight. Every meal tray thus includes a small card with the following biblical passage from Psalms: "I will praise God's name in song and glorify Him with Thanksgiving." I called the flight attendant over to ask where the card had come from and at first she seemed suspicious. It was only after I mentioned how much I had enjoyed it that she shared with me the number of passengers who had complained about it. She said there were very few who had a positive reaction to this prayer of thanksgiving. Personally, I can't think of a better place to praise God and give thanks than on an airline flight.

Living Abundantly

Being obedient to God's word also allows us to live abundant lives. According to the Bible, poverty is only a few days away. Proverbs 6:6–11 says, "Take a lesson from the ants, you lazy fellow. Learn from their ways and be wise. For they have no king to make them work, yet they labor hard all summer, gathering food for the winter. But you, all you do is sleep. Let me sleep a little longer! Sure just a little more. And as you sleep, poverty creeps upon you like a robber and destroys you; want attacks you in full armor."

Echoing this, a financial planner told me once that most Americans are only a paycheck away from bankruptcy. Spending is so high and debts so deep that missing even a couple of weeks of work without pay or losing one's job may mean losing everything.

Everyone knows that the harder they work, the luckier they get. Numerous passages in the Bible reflect this sentiment. Proverbs 10:4 states, "Lazy men are soon poor, hard workers get rich" while Proverbs 13:4 adds, "Lazy people want much but get little. But the diligent prosper." Proverbs 21:5 says simply, "Steady plodding brings prosperity; hasty speculation brings poverty."

Likewise, the more educated we become and the more goals we set and achieve, the more prosperous we become. The biblical basis for this philosophy has been around for centuries. It makes a lot of sense, but is it common sense? Look again at the lottery, which has taken hold of the fantasy and psyche of America.

A recent Powerball lottery game in New York boasted a jackpot of more than $150 million. Gamblers lined up for hundreds of yards at each store to buy tickets, even though the chances of winning were smaller than getting electrocuted in the bathtub.

Or consider Las Vegas, the fastest growing city in America. During the recession of 1991–1992, Vegas was the only city in the country with a positive economic growth rate. Its Mirage hotel cost nearly $800 million to build, yet it was paid for in cash within three months from the slot machine receipts. The Bellagio hotel cost more than one billion, yet it was paid for in six months with slot machine receipts.

One frequently hears that gambling is great entertainment, but if you knew you were going to return home two thousand dollars poorer than when you left, wouldn't it be wiser to take a trip to Hawaii or even invest your extra cash instead? Remember the wise old adage, "A fool and his money are soon parted."

Learning Obedience through Self-Discipline

D. L. Moody, the great evangelist, was once asked who among all the people he came into contact with gave him the most trouble. The questioner was thinking about the truly depraved, drunks, and prostitutes. Moody replied, "D. L. Moody. He gives me the most trouble." Another minister said, "If you could kick the person most responsible for your problems, you wouldn't be able to sit down for a week."

The word "self-discipline" might seem strange to use in the context of a spiritual walk with God, but all true self-discipline comes through the grace and mercy of God by faith. "Discipline" refers to a chastising or correcting that comes from an act of disobedience. If we're willing to learn, God teaches us the discipline necessary to stay obedient by also teaching us submissiveness. We submit to God most effectively when we have needs we want God to provide and problems we want God to solve. I learned this the hard way in 1990.

I was newly divorced as a result of breaking the rule God laid out of becoming equally yoked with another believer. I had married a woman who had cheated on her husband and then divorced him. She said she was a Christian, but she was really a cultural Christian. After a rocky seven years of marriage, she had another affair and filed for divorce from me. After two years of litigation, the court ordered me to pay alimony for one year and child support for our daughter.

The order was fair but the timing was not. In 1991, I was remarried and had a baby on the way. The recession of 1991 was in full swing and my business took a nosedive.

There was no way I could pay forty percent of my income to my ex-wife even in the best of times. I was depressed and prayed daily for help from the Lord. But in need comes submissiveness and dependence on God, which often results in trust and faith. Believing that God would solve my problems and deliver me from my troubles was difficult, but I chose to trust God no matter what and read story after story, book after book, about others who put their trust in God.

Joseph, for example, was sold into slavery by his brothers after he told them about the dream he'd had in which they were under his authority. Joseph was the son of Jacob, great-grandson of Abraham, and at the time Jacob's youngest and favorite child. According to the Bible, Joseph loved God and was obedient to God's word. He also had great faith and an amazing ability to interpret dreams.

After Joseph was sold into slavery, traders took him to Egypt and sold him to a government official named Potifar. Potifar's wife was attracted to Joseph and soon tried to seduce him.

I can hardly imagine what must have been going through Joseph's mind. Here was a young man in his sexual prime who had been deprived of all contact with women for years, rejecting the advances of his attractive employer. Joseph must have known that if he didn't do what his mistress wanted he would be punished. But engaging in sex with her would have gone against God's word to abstain from fornication and adultery.

As he was fleeing from her, Potifar's wife ripped part of Joseph's garment, which she used as evidence that Joseph had tried to rape her. She showed her husband the scrap of clothing as proof that he and she had been together. Surprisingly, Joseph wasn't killed, but he was sentenced to prison. He had been a prisoner for many years when Pharaoh had a dream that his spiritual advisors couldn't interpret. A cook who had been in prison remembered

Joseph's skill at interpreting dreams and suggested to Pharaoh that they ask his opinion. Joseph's interpretation of the dream came in the form of a prediction that Egypt would be filled with wealth and food for seven years, and after that would come seven years of famine.

Archeologists have recently discovered that this is more than just an ancient story. According to recent finds, the famine extended all the way to Yemen. A papyrus document was found with the writing of one wealthy Yemeni woman instructing her servant to give "Joseph, the leader in Egypt," twenty pieces of silver for as much wheat as her servant could buy.

I love this story because it shows that self-discipline and obedience to God's word results in blessings we could never have foreseen. God blesses those who keep His word. God blesses those who trust Him. During my marital and financial troubles, I needed to become submissive to God. I needed to learn to trust Him not just when times seemed bleak but also when times were good. I needed to depend on God's will for my life, which was actually much richer than I could ever have hoped for. I needed to not be my own worst enemy.

Self-discipline and obedience to God's word results in blessings we could never have foreseen.

It may sound harsh, but the difficulties and tribulations we experience are opportunities for us to learn how to be more submissive to God, to learn obedience through self-discipline. Some years ago, a good friend of mine was in the middle of a messy divorce. Leaving two small children, his wife ran off with her boss to San Diego. After a year, she sued for custody. Jeff was terrified the court would automatically assume a mother should have custody. He also worried that his former wife would take his kids many miles away to where she now lived with her new boyfriend.

Jeff couldn't bear the thought that he would only see his children every other weekend.

Jeff didn't know the Lord, yet I told him that God often brings trouble into our lives to get our attention focused on Him. He found that hard to believe and just wanted to find a good lawyer. I agreed with him that he needed legal help, but he also needed to look to God for help in what was the most trying time of his life.

Jeff and I often talked about God and I told him about Jesus's time on earth to show us how to gain salvation from sin. Finally, Jeff accepted God after an evening Bible study.

A self-disciplined life doesn't mean you will be bored with endless Bible studies and dates that end with only a handshake.

Do you think it's a coincidence that Jeff won custody of his kids or that he now is one of the wealthiest people in California like Joseph was in Egypt? The simple truth was that Jeff needed to trust God.

Don't fear that a strict adherence to God's word will make life boring and sacrificial. Jesus Christ said He came to show us how to live life more abundantly. A self-disciplined life doesn't mean you will be bored with endless Bible studies and dates that end with only a handshake. Following God's word means that you will be infinitely happier than if you chased happiness on your own worldly terms.

Applying the Techniques of Self-Discipline to Your Spiritual Walk with God

What facet of your relationship with God needs strengthening? Your prayer life? Your faith? Your thankfulness? Literally every chapter in this book contains techniques you can use to gain the self-discipline you need to strengthen your spiritual walk with God. Go down the list: You can assess your values, set goals, and concentrate on outcomes. You can use visualization and recasting. You can model the behavior of others. You can change your beliefs. You can use contracts. You can use meta patterns. You can learn to cope with the stress that strengthening your relationship with God may cause you. What follows are just a few of the specific techniques we've discussed:

Set Goals

Begin strengthening your spiritual walk with God by setting goals for yourself and the dates by which you want to achieve them. It could be that you want to take an hour each day to read your Bible and pray. You may also want to achieve this goal within thirty days. This is realistic, but you can't just start praying for an hour today and expect that behavior to last. It will be too abrupt a change in your life. You may manage it for a few days but then you will just stop. Instead, you should start out slowly, slicing the goal into small pieces initially and then into larger pieces until you've reached your goal.

Perhaps today you can start with ten minutes of prayer and reading. Next week, build up to fifteen minutes. Add fifteen more minutes a week to your daily prayer time, eventually building up to the hour you set as a goal in the beginning.

Use Pattern Interrupt

In an earlier chapter we discussed a self-discipline technique called pattern interrupt that entails wearing a rubber band around your wrist. When you feel anxious, you are to snap the rubber band to interrupt the anxiety you are feeling.

The same technique can be used to remind you to pray. When you feel anxious or angry or empty or even fearful, snap the rubber band. It will interrupt the pattern and will also remind you to pray.

Check Your S.U.D.S. Level

It may be hard to imagine folks who feel stress at the thought of walking into a house of worship, but the sad fact is that many people have troubling associations with attending church, for a variety of reasons. If you want to strengthen your spiritual walk by sharing in fellowship with other believers but you always seem to miss that Friday night Bible study while Sunday after Sunday goes by without you ever making it past your own front door, try checking your S.U.D.S. level to see how much stress you are under at the thought of going to church.

A next-door neighbor told me recently that he was made to attend church every Sunday as a child. While this may not seem like a bad idea, the middle-aged man said he just sat there week after week listening to a sermon he didn't understand and didn't care about. He was so bored that he vowed he would never set foot in a church again or make his family go.

The tragedy is, many churches today have wonderful youth programs designed to make learning about God fun for kids. But my neighbor was so negative, he wouldn't even set foot in a church. If you procrastinate going, you may feel the same way.

Progressive Relaxation

If indeed you find your S.U.D.S. level is high at the thought of attending church or praying but you really do want to overcome these feelings, use the technique we learned earlier called progressive relaxation. Imagine yourself at the top of the staircase taking a step down with every deep breath. As you walk, you will become more relaxed. When you reach the bottom step, your S.U.D.S. level will also be lower.

Immediate Rewards

You can also use the self-discipline technique of immediate rewards to deepen your relationship with God. For example, if you want to strengthen your children's relationship with God, try reading Bible stories to them at bedtime. There are Bible storybooks at every level. One of my daughters' favorites is the book called *Great Women of the Bible*. I want to encourage my girls not only in their spiritual walk with God but also in the knowledge that heroes of the Bible weren't just men. Thus, we read about Mary Magdalene who walked with Jesus, about Rachel who was married to Isaac, about Sarah, the wife of Abraham, and about Mary, the mother of Jesus. Using immediate rewards is how we get to bed early enough to read these great stories.

After I read to them, for example, I can watch my favorite TV program. The carrot to get my youngest into bed is to allow her a favorite drink, hot chocolate. She can drink it while I read to her but not until she hits the sack. So you see, you can reward your kids as well as yourself for being disciplined.

It's also important to avoid procrastination when it comes to teaching your children about God. The tendency might be to procrastinate because you think reading will take a long time or that your children won't enjoy it, but this is ridiculous. The stories are engaging and you can begin with just a single page.

Keep in mind too that one of the enemies of learning about God is the TV. Most programs are mindless and undermine the moral fabric of the family. Cutting out all but the most innocuous shows will go a long way toward making time to read to your kids and to talk about God.

Just remember: Self-discipline is more than getting yourself to work on time, losing weight, and completing projects. It is also the act of enabling you to stay close to God, whether you're interested in learning to trust in God, increasing your prayer time, or teaching your kids about God. Your spiritual walk is The Way to everlasting and eternal life. If you don't start drawing closer to God now, when will you?

ASSIGNMENTS
Putting Self-Discipline to Work

1. Prayer, reading the word of God, and obedience to God's word are central tenets in your spiritual walk. Accordingly, take time right now to set goals in each of these areas over the next weeks and months.
2. Try to apply the immediate and deferred rewards system to prayer and reading God's word every day this week. For example, don't drink your first cup of coffee in the morning until you have first prayed and read at least one chapter of the Bible. If you are a night person, don't watch TV in the evening until you have first spent time with God. Take time at the end of the week to treat yourself and a loved one to a special activity for completing the goals you've assigned to yourself.
3. Repentance of sin is central to allowing God to work in your life. The Bible says that the Holy Spirit grieves at our sin. What are you doing right now that would prevent you from proudly walking with God? What can you do to change this behavior?